Heavenly Cross-Stitch
Designs with a Christian Theme

Marie Barber

Sterling Publishing Co., Inc. New York
A Sterling/Chapelle Book

For Chapelle Limited

Owner: Jo Packham

Editor: Ann Bear

Staff: Areta Bingham, Kass Burchett, Rebecca Christensen, Holly Fuller, Marilyn Goff, Shirley Heslop, Holly Hollingsworth, Sherry Hoppe, Shawn Hsu, Susan Jorgensen, Pauline Locke, Barbara Milburn, Linda Orton, Karmen Quinney, Leslie Ridenour, Cindy Stoeckl

Photography: Kevin Dilley, Photographer for Hazen Photography
Photo Stylist: Jo Packham

We would like to offer our sincere appreciation of the valuable support given in this ever changing industry of new ideas, concepts, designs, and products. Several projects shown in this publication were created with the outstanding and innovative products developed by:
- **Anchor**; 30 Patewood Dr., Ste. 351; Greenville, S.C. 29615
- **Charles Craft**
- **DMC**; 10 Port Kearney Building; South Kearney, N.J. 07032-4688
- **Gay Bowles Sales, Mill Hill Beads**; P.O. Box 1060; Janesville, WI 53547; 1-800-356-9438
- **Krenick**; 3106 Timanus Lane, Ste. 101; Baltimore, MD 21244; 1-800-537-2166
- **Wichelt**; N 162 Hwy 35; Stoddard, WI 54658; 1-608-788-4600
- **Zweigart-Joan Taggart Ltd.**; 2 Riverview Dr.; Somerset, N.J. 08873; www.zweigart.com; email-info@zweigrt.com

If you have any questions or comments, please contact:

Chapelle, Ltd., Inc.
P.O. Box 9252
Ogden, UT 84409
(801) 621-2777
(801) 621-2788 Fax
chapelle1@aol.com

Due to the limited amount of space available, we must print our patterns at a reduced size in order to give our patrons the maximum number of patterns possible in our publications. We believe the quality and quantity of our patterns will compensate for any inconvenience this may cause.

Every effort has been made to ensure that all information in this book is accurate. However, due to differing conditions, tools, and individual skills, the publisher cannot be responsible for any injuries, losses, and other damages which may result from the use of the information in this book.

Library of Congress Cataloging-in-Publication Data Available

A Sterling/Chapelle Book

10 9 8 7 6 5 4 3 2 1

First paperback edition published in 1999 by
Sterling Publishing Company, Inc.
387 Park Avenue South, New York, N.Y. 10016
Produced by Chapelle Ltd.
P.O. Box 9252, Newgate Station, Ogden, Utah 84409
© 1998 by Chapelle Ltd.
Distributed in Canada by Sterling Publishing
℅ Canadian Manda Group, One Atlantic Avenue, Suite 105
Toronto, Ontario, Canada M6K 3E7
Distributed in Great Britain and Europe by Cassell PLC
Wellington House, 125 Strand, London WC2R 0BB England
Distributed in Australia by Capricorn Link (Australia) Pty Ltd.
P.O. Box 6651, Baulkham Hills, Business Centre, NSW 2153, Australia
Printed in Hong Kong
All rights reserved

Sterling ISBN 0-8069-0349-X Trade
              0-8069-2023-8 Paper

About the Author

Marie Barber, born and raised in Kristianstad, Sweden, now lives in Ragland, Alabama, on the Coosa River with her husband and their two children.

Marie says she has always loved to draw and illustrate. At the age of 14, she was the youngest student to study oil painting under the instruction of the late Dr. Göran Trönnberg.

She came to the United States in 1983 as an exchange student, and in 1987, returned after being accepted to the Art Institute of Atlanta. She has freelanced as a novel illustrator for a Swedish weekly publication and her artwork is featured at Loretta Goodwin's Gallery in Birmingham, Alabama. Although she has explored several avenues of the art world, Marie says she found her passion in 1993 when she began designing cross-stitch patterns.

Table of Contents

General Instructions

Introduction
Contained in this book are 118 counted cross-stitch designs, including 90 miniature cross-stitch designs.

The mini-designs have been graphed in sampler form, but may be stitched either individually or as the sampler. Included for every design is a photograph of the completed work. However, photographs of some of the mini-designs are not included, in order to include as many graphed designs as possible. Each graphed design includes its own color code.

Fabric for Cross-stitch
Counted cross-stitch is worked on even-weave fabrics. These fabrics are manufactured specifically for counted-thread embroidery, and are woven with the same number of vertical as horizontal threads per inch.

Because the number of threads in the fabric is equal in each direction, each stitch will be the same size. The number of threads per inch in even-weave fabrics determines the size of a finished design.

Number of Strands
The number of strands used per stitch varies depending on the fabric used. Generally, the rule to follow for cross-stitching is three strands on Aida 11, two strands on Aida 14, one or two strands on Aida 18 (depending on desired thickness of stitches), and one strand on Hardanger 22.

For backstitching, use one strand on all fabrics. When completing a french knot, use two strands and one wrap on all fabrics, unless otherwise directed.

Preparing Fabric
Cut fabric at least 3" larger on all sides than finished design size to ensure enough space for desired assembly. If the design is used to embellish a project that will be finished further, check instructions for specific fabric allowances.

To prevent fraying, whipstitch or machine-zigzag along raw edges or apply liquid fray preventer.

Needles for Cross-stitch
Blunt needles should slip easily through fabric holes without piercing fabric threads. For fabric with 11 or fewer threads per inch, use a tapestry needle size 24; for 14 threads per inch, use a tapestry needle size 24 or 26; for 18 or more threads per inch, use a tapestry needle size 26. Never leave needle in design area of fabric. It may leave rust or a permanent impression on fabric.

Finished Design Size
To determine size of finished design, divide stitch count by number of threads per inch of fabric. When design is stitched over two threads, divide stitch count by half the threads per inch. For example, if a design with a stitch count of 120 width and 250 length were stitched on a 28 count linen over two threads, the end size would be 8⅝" x 17⅞".

Floss
All numbers and color names on the codes represent DMC and Anchor brands of floss. Use 18" lengths of floss. For best coverage, separate strands. Dampen with a wet sponge. Then put together the number of strands required for fabric used.

Centering the Design
Fold the fabric in half horizontally, then vertically. Place a pin in the fold point to mark the center. Locate the center of the design on the graph. To help in centering the samplers, arrows are provided at left-side center and bottom center. Begin stitching all designs at the center point of graph and fabric.

Securing the Floss
Insert needle up from the underside of the fabric at starting point. Hold 1" of thread behind the fabric and stitch over it, securing with the first few stitches. To finish thread, run under four or more stitches on the back of the design. Never knot floss, unless working on clothing.

Another method of securing floss is the waste knot. Knot floss and insert needle down from the right top side of the fabric about 1" from design area. Work several stitches over the thread to secure. Cut off the knot later.

Carrying Floss
To carry floss, weave floss under the previously worked stitches on the back. Do not carry thread across any fabric that is not or will not be stitched. Loose threads, especially dark ones, will show through the fabric.

Cleaning Finished Design
When stitching is finished, soak fabric in cold water with a mild soap for five to ten minutes. Rinse well and roll in a towel to remove excess water. Do not wring. Place work face down on

a dry towel and iron on warm setting until the fabric is dry.

Cross-stitch
Stitches are done in a row or, if necessary, one at a time in an area.
1. Insert needle up between woven threads at A.
2. Go down at B, the hole diagonally across from A.
3. Come back up at C and down at D, etc.
4. To complete the top stitches creating an "X", come up at E and go down at B, come up at C and go down at F, etc. All top stitches should lie in the same direction.

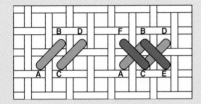

Backstitch
1. Insert needle up between woven threads at A.
2. Go down at B, one opening to the right.
3. Come back up at C.
4. Go down one opening to the right, this time at A.

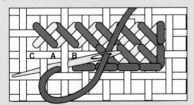

French Knot
1. Insert needle up between woven threads at A, using two strands of embroidery floss.
2. Loosely wrap floss once around needle.
3. Go down at B, the hole diagonally across from A. Pull floss taut as needle is pushed down through fabric.
4. Carry floss across back of work between knots.

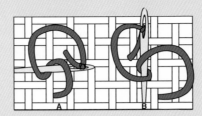

Long Stitch
1. Insert needle up between woven threads at A.
2. Go down at B. Pull flat. Repeat A–B for each stitch. Stitch may be horizontal, verticle, or diagonal as indicated in examples 1, 2, and 3. The length of the stitch should be the same as the length indicated on the graph.

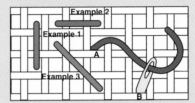

Continental Stitch
Stitches are done in a row working from right to left or top to bottom in vertical columns.
1. Insert needle up between woven threads at A.
2. Go down at B, the hole diagonally across from A.
3. Come back up at C and down at D, etc. The back side of stitching will result in long verticle stitches.

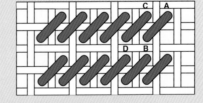

Bead Attachment
Beads should sit facing the same direction as the top cross-stitch.
1. Make first half of a cross-stitch.
2. Insert needle up between woven threads at A.
3. Pick up one bead before going down at B, the hole diagonally across from A.

4. To strengthen stitch, come up again at A and either go through bead again or split threads to lay around bead and go down at B again.

Wrapped Backstitch
1. Refer to Backstitch. Complete backstitches.
2. Insert needle up between woven threads at A.
3. Wrap over first stitch.
4. Go under second stitch. Be careful not to pierce the fabric or catch the backstitch.
5. Come up on the opposite side of the stitch at B. Continue the length of the backstitching. The effect can be varied by how loosely or tightly the floss is pulled when wrapping.

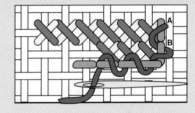

Satin Stitch
1. Insert needle up between woven threads at A.
2. Go down at B, forming a straight stitch.
3. Come up at C and go down at D, forming another smooth straight stitch that is slightly overlapping the first.
4. Repeat to fill design area.

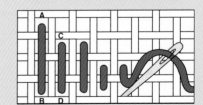

5

Cathedral Glass

The sample was stitched on Antique White Cashel Linen 28 over 2. The finished design size is 8⅝" x 17⅞". The fabric was cut 15" x 24".

Anchor **DMC**

Step 1: Cross-stitch (2 strands)

Anchor		DMC	
1			White
926			Ecru
386		746	Off White (1 strand)
300		745	Yellow–lt. pale (1 strand)
293		727	Topaz–vy. lt.
306		725	Topaz (1 strand)
307		783	Christmas Gold (1 strand)
891		676	Old Gold–lt.
890		729	Old Gold–med. (1 strand)
307		783	Christmas Gold (1 strand)
308		782	Topaz–med.
886		3047	Yellow Beige–lt.
881		945	Peach Beige
4146		950	Peach Pecan–dk. (1 strand)
882		3773	Pecan–vy. lt. (1 strand)
882		3773	Pecan–vy. lt.
892		225	Shell Pink– vy. lt.
969		3727	Antique Mauve–lt. (1 strand)
95		554	Violet–lt. (1 strand)
42		309	Rose–deep (1 strand)
98		553	Violet–med. (1 strand)
108		211	Lavender–lt. (1 strand)
869		3743	Antique Violet–vy. lt. (1 strand)
105		209	Lavender–dk.
110		208	Lavender–vy. dk. (1 strand)
101		327	Antique Violet–vy. dk. (1 strand)
870		3042	Antique Violet–lt.
117		3747	Blue Violet–lt.
121		794	Cornflower Blue–lt.
940		793	Cornflower Blue–med. (1 strand)
941		3807	Cornflower Blue (1 strand)
158		775	Baby Blue–vy. lt.
159		3325	Baby Blue–lt. (1 strand)
130		799	Delft–med. (1 strand)
130		799	Delft–med. (1 strand)
978		322	Navy Blue–vy. lt. (1 strand)
147		312	Navy Blue–lt.
160		3761	Sky Blue–lt.
264		772	Pine Green–lt. (1 strand)
265		3348	Yellow Green–lt. (1 strand)
266		3347	Yellow Green–med. (1 strand)
779		926	Slate Green (1 strand)
840		3768	Slate Green–dk. (1 strand)
851		924	Slate Green–vy. dk. (1 strand)
309		435	Brown–vy. lt. (1 strand)
379		840	Beige Brown–med. (1 strand)
887		372	Mustard–lt.
898		611	Drab Brown–dk.
905		3781	Mocha Brown–dk.
905		3781	Mocha Brown–dk. (1 strand)
382		3371	Black Brown (1 strand)
399		451	Shell Gray–dk.
399		451	Shell Gray–dk. (1 strand)
872		3740	Antique Violet–dk. (1 strand)
263		3799	Pewter Gray–vy. dk. (1 strand)
101		327	Antique Violet–vy. dk. (1 strand)
403		310	Black

Step 2: Backstitch (1 strand)

Anchor		DMC	
382		3371	Black Brown
403		310	Black

Step 3: French Knot (1 strand)

Anchor		DMC	
382		3371	Black Brown

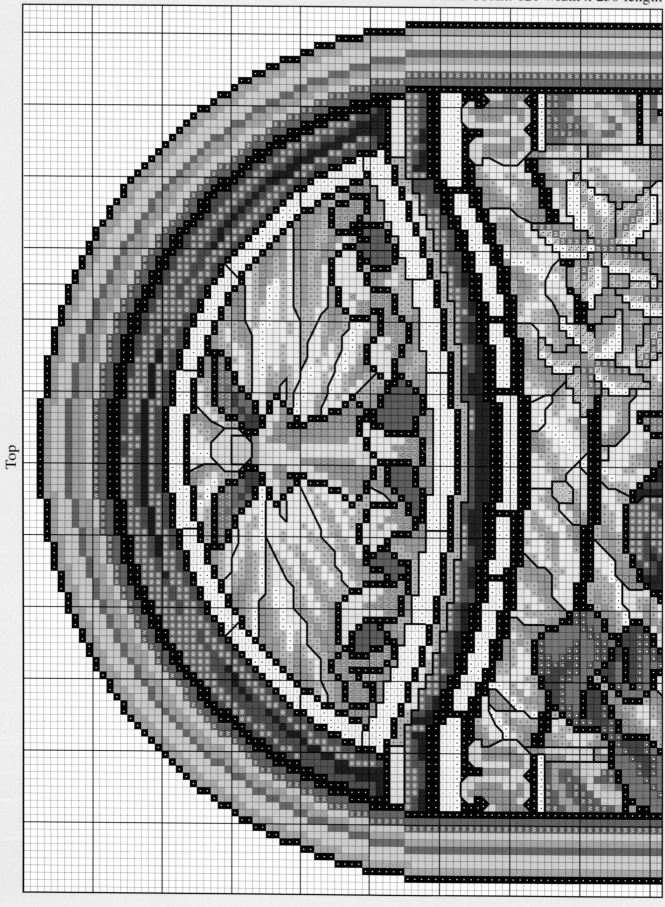

Top

Middle

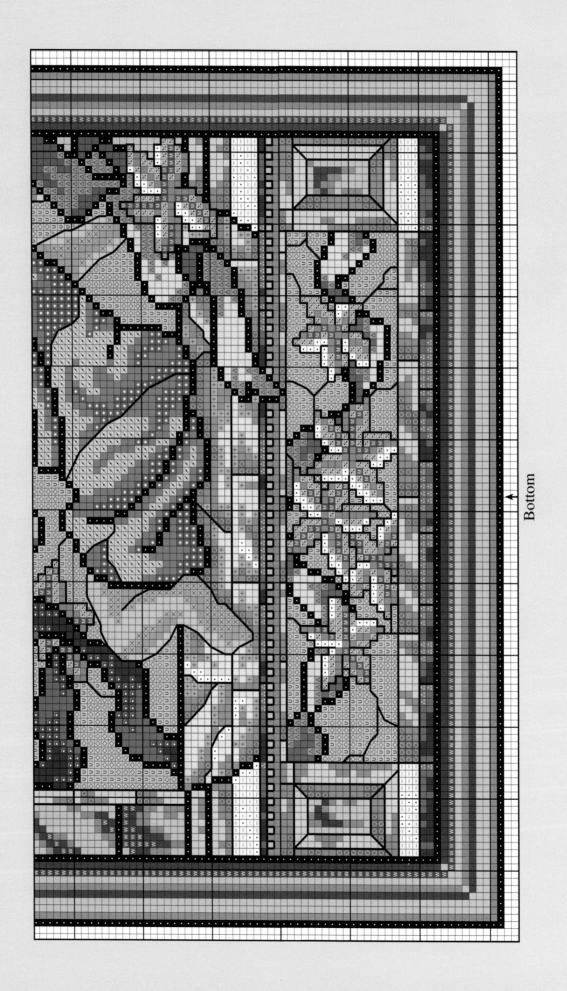

Bottom

Celestial Melody

The sample was stitched on Dirty Linen Cashel Linen 28 over 2. The finished design size is 6¾" x 6¾". The fabric was cut 13" x 13".

Anchor   **DMC**

Step 1: Cross-stitch (2 strands)

Anchor		DMC	
1	·		White
300	×	745	Yellow–lt. pale
886		677	Old Gold–vy. lt.
886	–	677	Old Gold–vy. lt. (1 strand)
1			White (1 strand)
891		676	Old Gold–lt.
373		3045	Yellow Beige–dk.
10		352	Coral–lt.
8	△	761	Salmon–lt.
10	H	3712	Salmon–med.
897		221	Shell Pink–vy. dk.
5975		356	Terra Cotta–med.
5975		356	Terra Cotta–med. (1 strand)
5968		355	Terra Cotta–vy. dk. (1 strand)
1014	❋	3830	Terra Cotta
160		813	Blue–lt.
920	⋰	932	Antique Blue–lt. (1 strand)
921		931	Antique Blue–med. (1 strand)
921		931	Antique Blue–med. (1 strand)
922		930	Antique Blue–dk. (1 strand)
849		927	Slate Green–med.
213		369	Pistachio Green–vy. lt. (1 strand)
265		3348	Yellow Green–lt. (1 strand)
861	O	3363	Pine Green–med.
860		3053	Green Gray
859	⋰	3052	Green Gray–med.
879	E	500	Blue Green–vy. dk. (1 strand)
861		3363	Pine Green–med. (1 strand)
868		758	Terra Cotta–lt. (1 strand)
933		3774	Peach Pecan–med. (1 strand)
868	✚	758	Terra Cotta–lt. (1 strand)
860		3053	Green Gray (1 strand)
868		758	Terra Cotta–lt. (1 strand)
338		3776	Mahogany–lt. (1 strand)
914		3064	Pecan–lt.
933		3774	Peach Pecan–med.
933	✓	3774	Peach Pecan–med. (1 strand)
1			White (1 strand)
914	K	3772	Pecan–med. (1 strand)
10		352	Coral–lt. (1 strand)
914	★	3772	Pecan–med. (1 strand)
5968		355	Terra Cotta–vy. dk. (1 strand)
914	N	3772	Pecan–med. (1 strand)
363		436	Tan (1 strand)
936		632	Pecan–dk.
388		3033	Mocha Brown–vy. lt.
956	S	613	Drab Brown–lt.
956	·1	613	Drab Brown–lt. (1 strand)
8581		646	Beaver Gray–dk. (1 strand)
373		422	Hazel Nut Brown–lt.
889	Z	370	Mustard–med.
889	∴	370	Mustard–med. (1 strand)
921		931	Antique Blue–med. (1 strand)
347	▽	402	Mahogany–vy. lt.
347	G	402	Mahogany–vy. lt. (1 strand)
886		677	Old Gold–vy. lt. (1 strand)
338	W	3776	Mahogany–lt.
942	◇	738	Tan–vy. lt.
363	✚	436	Tan
363	U	436	Tan (1 strand)
891		676	Old Gold–lt. (1 strand)
379		840	Beige Brown–med.
381		838	Beige Brown–vy. dk. (1 strand)
936		632	Pecan–dk. (1 strand)
8581	M	646	Beaver Gray–dk.
273	B	3787	Brown Gray–dk. (1 strand)
846		3051	Green Gray–dk. (1 strand)
401	♥	844	Beaver Gray–ultra dk.
397		762	Pearl Gray–vy. lt.
397	✗	762	Pearl Gray–vy. lt. (1 strand)
343		3752	Antique Blue–vy. lt. (1 strand)
403		310	Black (1 strand)
879		500	Blue Green–vy. dk. (1 strand)
403	■	310	Black

Step 2: Backstitch (1 strand)

381	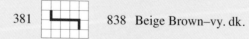	838	Beige Brown–vy. dk.

Step 3: Long Stitch (1 strand)

936		632	Pecan–dk.

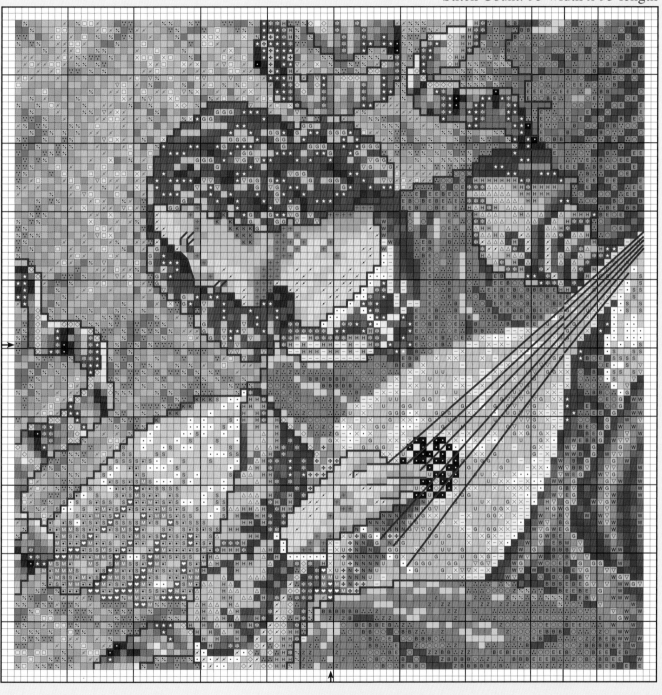

Cherubic Garden

The sample was stitched on Antique White Cashel Linen 28 over 2. The finished design size is 14" x 11". The fabric was cut 20" x 17".

Anchor   **DMC**

Step 1:   Cross-stitch (2 strands)

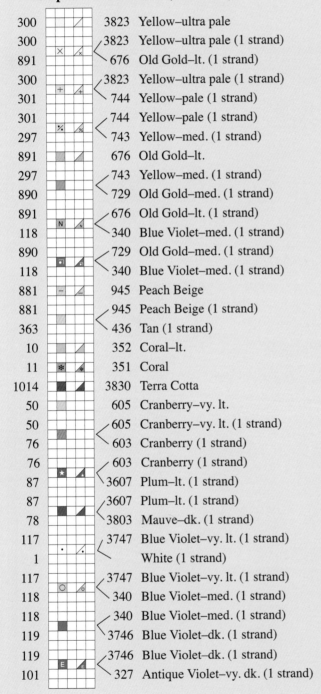

Anchor	DMC	
300	3823	Yellow–ultra pale
300	3823	Yellow–ultra pale (1 strand)
891	676	Old Gold–lt. (1 strand)
300	3823	Yellow–ultra pale (1 strand)
301	744	Yellow–pale (1 strand)
301	744	Yellow–pale (1 strand)
297	743	Yellow–med. (1 strand)
891	676	Old Gold–lt.
297	743	Yellow–med. (1 strand)
890	729	Old Gold–med. (1 strand)
891	676	Old Gold–lt. (1 strand)
118	340	Blue Violet–med. (1 strand)
890	729	Old Gold–med. (1 strand)
118	340	Blue Violet–med. (1 strand)
881	945	Peach Beige
881	945	Peach Beige (1 strand)
363	436	Tan (1 strand)
10	352	Coral–lt.
11	351	Coral
1014	3830	Terra Cotta
50	605	Cranberry–vy. lt.
50	605	Cranberry–vy. lt. (1 strand)
76	603	Cranberry (1 strand)
76	603	Cranberry (1 strand)
87	3607	Plum–lt. (1 strand)
87	3607	Plum–lt. (1 strand)
78	3803	Mauve–dk. (1 strand)
117	3747	Blue Violet–vy. lt. (1 strand)
1		White (1 strand)
117	3747	Blue Violet–vy. lt. (1 strand)
118	340	Blue Violet–med. (1 strand)
118	340	Blue Violet–med. (1 strand)
119	3746	Blue Violet–dk. (1 strand)
119	3746	Blue Violet–dk. (1 strand)
101	327	Antique Violet–vy. dk. (1 strand)

Anchor	DMC	
101	327	Antique Violet–vy. dk. (1 strand)
944	869	Hazel Nut Brown–vy. dk. (1 strand)
158	3756	Baby Blue–ultra vy. lt.
158	3756	Baby Blue–ultra vy. lt. (1 strand)
343	3752	Antique Blue–vy. lt. (1 strand)
343	3752	Antique Blue–vy. lt.
343	3752	Antique Blue–vy. lt. (1 strand)
160	813	Blue–lt. (1 strand)
264	472	Avocado Green–ultra lt.
264	472	Avocado Green–ultra lt. (1 strand)
266	581	Moss Green (1 strand)
257	3346	Hunter Green
257	3346	Hunter Green (1 strand)
879	500	Blue Green–vy. dk. (1 strand)
279	734	Olive Green–lt.
280	733	Olive Green–med.
889	831	Olive Green
843	3364	Pine Green
861	3363	Pine Green–med.
861	3363	Pine Green–med. (1 strand)
879	500	Blue Green–vy. dk. (1 strand)
363	436	Tan
363	436	Tan (1 strand)
944	869	Hazel Nut Brown–vy. dk. (1 strand)

Step 2:   Backstitch (1 strand)

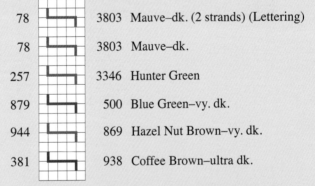

Anchor	DMC	
78	3803	Mauve–dk. (2 strands) (Lettering)
78	3803	Mauve–dk.
257	3346	Hunter Green
879	500	Blue Green–vy. dk.
944	869	Hazel Nut Brown–vy. dk.
381	938	Coffee Brown–ultra dk.

Step 3:   Long Stitch (2 strands)

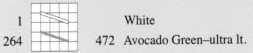

Anchor	DMC	
1		White
264	472	Avocado Green–ultra lt.

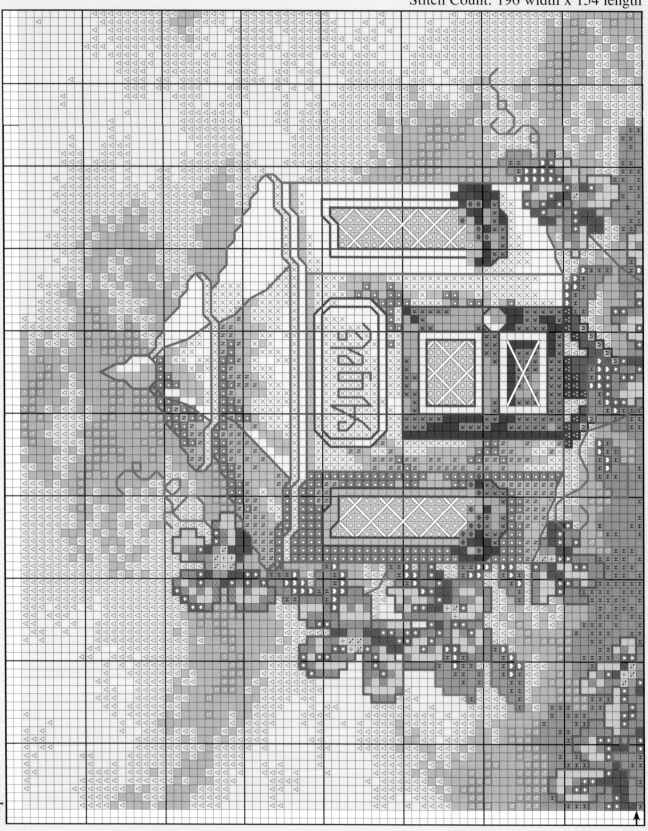

Top Left

Top Right

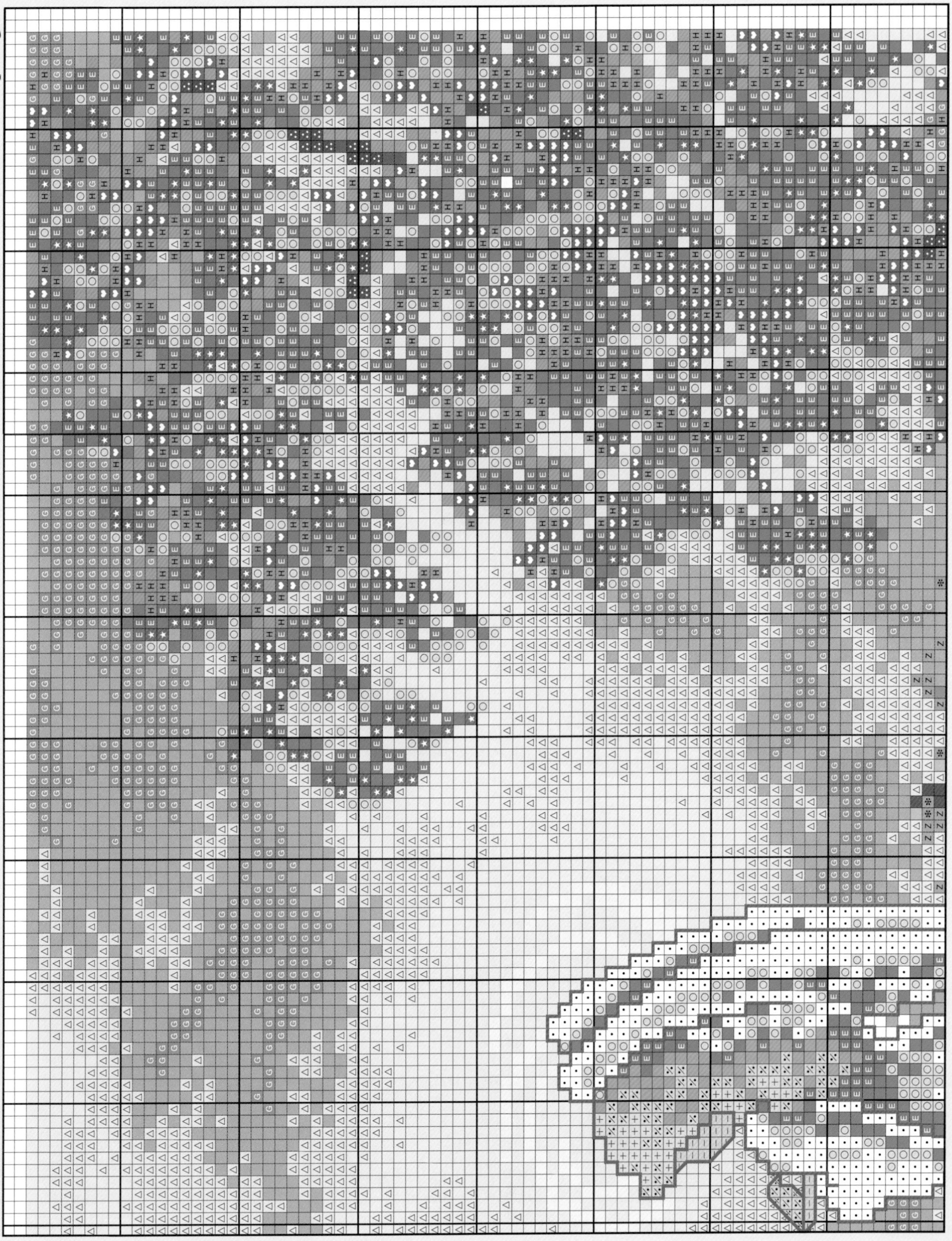

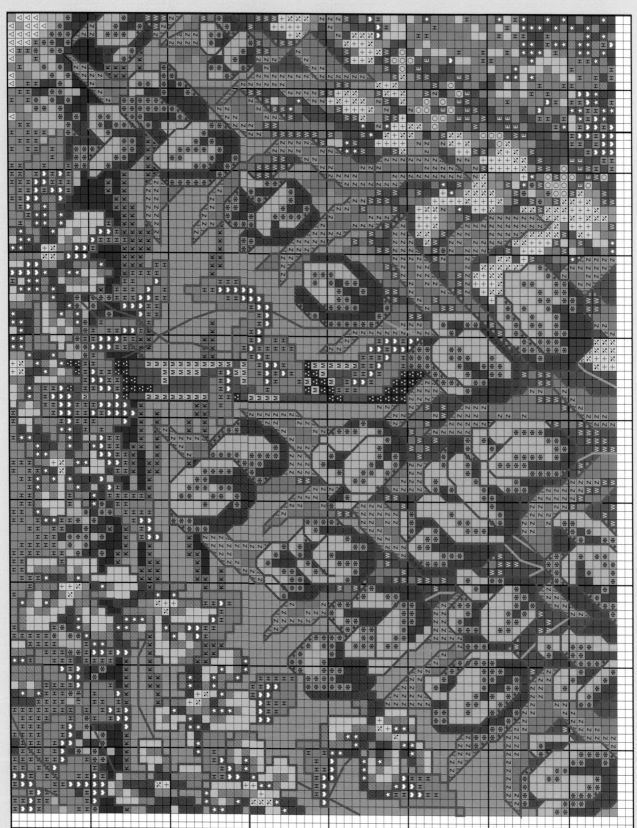

Bottom Left

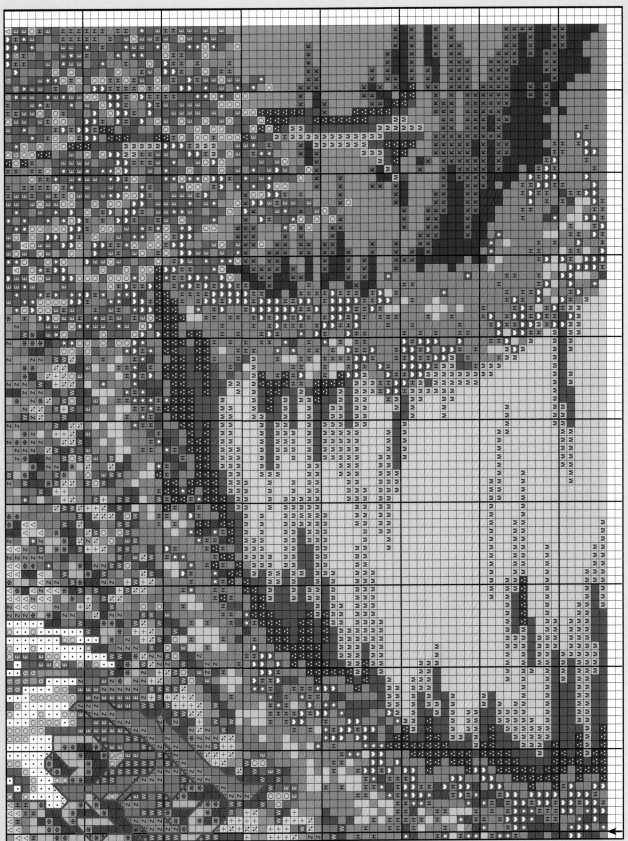

The Road to Bethlehem

The sample was stitched on Vintage Linen 28 over 2. The finished design size is 6⅛" x 4⅝". The fabric was cut 13" x 11".

Anchor   DMC

Step 1:   Cross-stitch (2 strands)

Anchor		DMC	
387		712	Cream
886		677	Old Gold–vy. lt.
887		3046	Yellow Beige–med.
301		744	Yellow–pale
307		783	Christmas Gold
881		945	Peach Beige
86		3608	Plum–vy. lt.
87		3607	Plum–lt.
78		3803	Mauve–dk.
104		210	Lavender–med. (1 strand)
118		340	Blue Violet–med. (1 strand)
118		340	Blue Violet–med.
158		775	Baby Blue–vy. lt.
159		827	Blue–vy. lt.
121		793	Cornflower Blue–med.
940		792	Cornflower Blue–dk.
779		926	Slate Green
779		926	Slate Green (1 strand)
922		930	Antique Blue–dk. (1 strand)
213		504	Blue Green–lt.
264		472	Avocado Green–ultra lt.
844		3012	Khaki Green–med.
844		3012	Khaki Green–med. (1 strand)
846		3051	Green Gray–dk. (1 strand)
363		436	Tan
832		612	Drab Brown–med.
830		644	Beige Gray–med.
392		642	Beige Gray–dk.
903		640	Beige Gray–vy. dk. (1 strand)
382		3021	Brown Gray–vy. dk. (1 strand)
382		3021	Brown Gray–vy. dk. (1 strand)
236		3799	Pewter Gray–vy. dk. (1 strand)

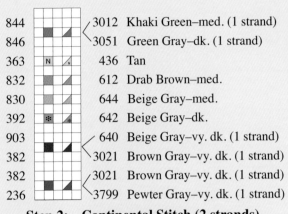

Step 2:   Continental Stitch (2 strands)

Anchor		DMC	
301		744	Yellow–pale
104		210	Lavender–med. (1 strand)
118		340	Blue Violet–med. (1 strand)
846		3051	Green Gray–dk.
373		422	Hazel Nut Brown–lt.
307		977	Golden Brown–lt.
382		3021	Brown Gray–vy. dk.

Step 3:   Backstitch (1 strand)

Anchor		DMC	
307		783	Christmas Gold (2 strands)
872		3740	Antique Violet–dk.
382		3021	Brown Gray–vy. dk.

Step 4:   Long Stitch (2 strands)

Anchor		DMC	
387		712	Cream

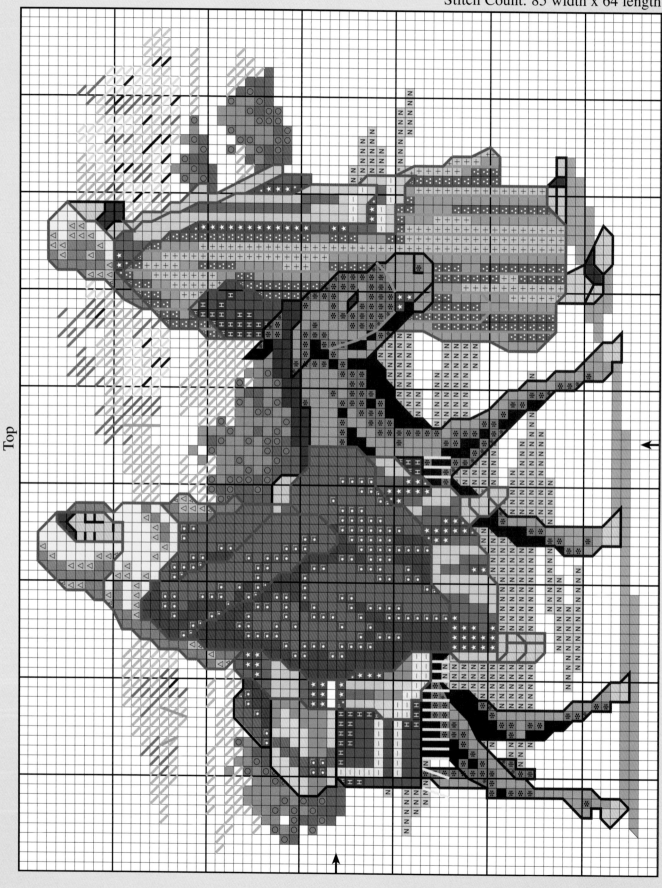

Top

Three Wise Men

The sample was stitched on Smokey Pearl Cashel Linen 28 over 2. The finished design size is 5⅜" x 7⅞". The fabric was cut 12" x 14".

Anchor   **DMC**

Step 1: Cross-stitch (2 strands)

Anchor		DMC	
387		712	Cream
300		3823	Yellow–ultra pale
305		3822	Straw–lt.
301		744	Yellow–pale
4146		754	Peach–lt.
50		3716	Wild Rose–lt.
69		3687	Mauve
78		3803	Mauve–dk.
86		3608	Plum–vy. lt.
87		3607	Plum–lt. (1 strand)
105		209	Lavender–dk. (1 strand)
88		718	Plum (1 strand)
99		552	Violet–dk. (1 strand)
872		3740	Antique Violet–dk.
928		3811	Turquoise–vy. lt.
168		807	Peacock Blue
168		807	Peacock Blue (1 strand)
1066		3809	Turquoise–vy. dk. (1 strand)
1066		3809	Turquoise–vy. dk. (1 strand)
149		311	Navy Blue–med.(1 strand)
130		799	Delft–med.
978		322	Navy Blue–vy. lt.
162		824	Blue–dk.

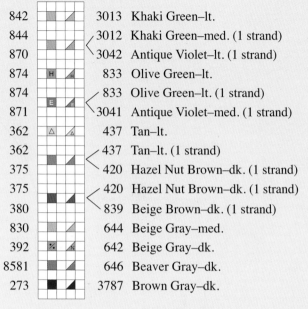

Anchor		DMC	
842		3013	Khaki Green–lt.
844		3012	Khaki Green–med. (1 strand)
870		3042	Antique Violet–lt. (1 strand)
874		833	Olive Green–lt.
874		833	Olive Green–lt. (1 strand)
871		3041	Antique Violet–med. (1 strand)
362		437	Tan–lt.
362		437	Tan–lt. (1 strand)
375		420	Hazel Nut Brown–dk. (1 strand)
375		420	Hazel Nut Brown–dk. (1 strand)
380		839	Beige Brown–dk. (1 strand)
830		644	Beige Gray–med.
392		642	Beige Gray–dk.
8581		646	Beaver Gray–dk.
273		3787	Brown Gray–dk.

Step 2: Backstitch (1 strand)

Anchor		DMC	
872		3740	Antique Violet–dk.
149		311	Navy Blue–med.
874		833	Olive Green–lt. (2 strands)
375		420	Hazel Nut Brown–dk.
380		839	Beige Brown–dk.
273		3787	Brown Gray–dk.

Step 3: French Knot (1 strand)

Anchor		DMC	
872		3740	Antique Violet–dk.
149		311	Navy Blue–med.

Mary & the Christ Child

The sample was stitched on Platinum Dublin Linen 25 over 2. The finished design size is 9¼" x 12⅝". The fabric was cut 16" x 19".

Anchor	DMC	

Step 1: Cross-stitch (2 strands)

Anchor	DMC	
1		White
386	3823	Yellow–ultra pale
300	745	Yellow–lt. pale
891	676	Old Gold–lt.
891	676	Old Gold–lt. (1 strand)
386	3823	Yellow–ultra pale (1 strand)
366	951	Peach Pecan–lt.
881	945	Peach Beige
881	945	Peach Beige (1 strand)
868	758	Terra Cotta–lt. (1 strand)
48	818	Baby Pink
8	761	Salmon–lt.
9	760	Salmon
892	225	Shell Pink–vy. lt.
893	224	Shell Pink–lt.
893	224	Shell Pink–lt. (1 strand)
894	223	Shell Pink–med. (1 strand)
896	3722	Shell Pink
896	3722	Shell Pink (1 strand)
9	760	Salmon (1 strand)
108	211	Lavender–lt.
108	211	Lavender–lt. (1 strand)
105	209	Lavender–dk. (1 strand)
105	209	Lavender–dk.

Anchor	DMC	
105	209	Lavender–dk. (1 strand)
871	3041	Antique Violet–med. (1 strand)
870	3042	Antique Violet–lt.
871	3041	Antique Violet–med.
870	3042	Antique Violet–lt. (1 strand)
117	3747	Blue Violet–vy. lt. (1 strand)
117	3747	Blue Violet–vy. lt. (1 strand)
1		White (1 strand)
347	402	Mahogany–vy. lt.
338	3776	Mahogany–lt.
387	822	Beige Gray–lt.
874	834	Olive Green–vy. lt.
944	869	Hazel Nut Brown–vy. dk.
956	613	Drab Brown–lt. (1 strand)
387	822	Beige Gray–lt. (1 strand)
956	613	Drab Brown–lt.
898	611	Drab Brown–dk. (1 strand)
891	676	Old Gold–lt. (1 strand)

Step 2: Backstitch (1 strand)

Anchor	DMC	
896	3722	Shell Pink
1019	3802	Antique Mauve–deep
871	3041	Antique Violet–med.
874	834	Olive Green–vy. lt.
944	869	Hazel Nut Brown–vy. dk.
956	613	Drab Brown–lt. (2 strands)
898	611	Drab Brown–dk.

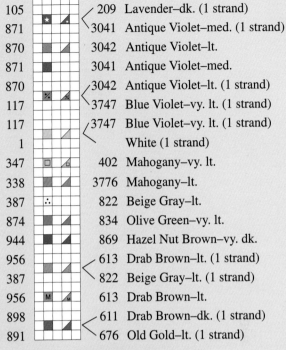

Glory to God in the highest, and on earth peace, good will toward men. -- Luke 2:14

Top

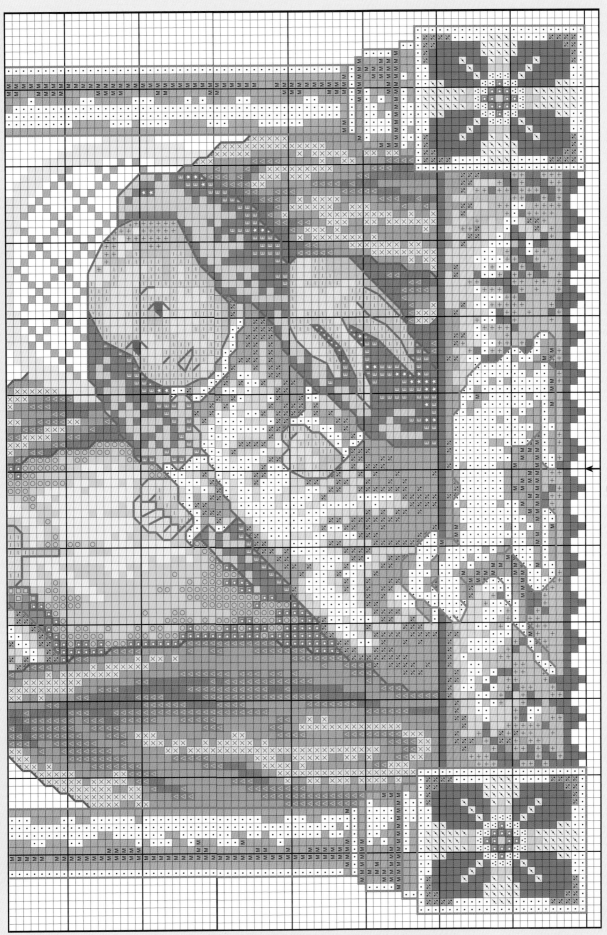

Bottom

29

Jesus & the Children

The sample was stitched on Antique White Cashel Linen 28 over 2. The finished design size is 7⅞" x 13⅝". The fabric was cut 14" x 20".

Anchor   **DMC**

Step 1:   Cross-stitch (2 strands)

Anchor	DMC	Color
1		White
886	677	Old Gold–vy. lt.
891	676	Old Gold–lt.
366	951	Peach Pecan–lt.
4146	950	Peach Pecan–dk.
4146	950	Peach Pecan–dk. (1 strand)
882	3773	Pecan–vy. lt. (1 strand)
50	3716	Wild Rose–lt. (1 strand)
969	3727	Antique Mauve–lt. (1 strand)
75	3733	Dusty Rose–lt. (1 strand)
969	316	Antique Mauve–med. (1 strand)
69	3687	Mauve (1 strand)
970	3726	Antique Mauve–dk. (1 strand)
968	778	Antique Mauve–vy. lt.
969	3727	Antique Mauve–lt.
969	316	Antique Mauve–med.
969	316	Antique Mauve–med. (1 strand)
970	3726	Antique Mauve–dk. (1 strand)
970	3726	Antique Mauve–dk.
970	315	Antique Mauve–vy. dk.
869	3743	Antique Violet–vy. lt.
869	3743	Antique Violet–vy. lt. (1 strand)
117	3747	Blue Violet–vy. lt. (1 strand)
870	3042	Antique Violet–lt. (1 strand)
117	341	Blue Violet–lt. (1 strand)
871	3041	Antique Violet–med. (1 strand)
118	340	Blue Violet–med. (1 strand)
876	3740	Antique Violet–dk. (1 strand)
119	3746	Blue Violet–dk. (1 strand)
117	3747	Blue Violet–vy. lt.
117	3747	Blue Violet–vy. lt. (1 strand)
117	341	Blue Violet–lt. (1 strand)
117	341	Blue Violet–lt.
121	794	Cornflower Blue–dk.
121	793	Cornflower Blue–med.
121	793	Cornflower Blue–med. (1 strand)
940	792	Cornflower Blue–dk. (1 strand)
940	792	Cornflower Blue–dk. (1 strand)
876	3740	Antique Violet–dk. (1 strand)
858	524	Fern Green–vy. lt. (1 strand)
213	504	Blue Green–lt. (1 strand)
859	523	Fern Green–lt. (1 strand)
875	503	Blue Green–med. (1 strand)
859	522	Fern Green (1 strand)
876	502	Blue Green (1 strand)
875	503	Blue Green–med.
876	502	Blue Green
878	501	Blue Green–dk.
878	501	Blue Green–dk. (1 strand)
840	3768	Slate Green–dk. (1 strand)
879	500	Blue Green–vy. dk.
347	402	Mahogany–vy. lt.
338	3776	Mahogany–lt.
349	301	Mahogany–med.
888	3828	Hazel Nut Brown
885	739	Tan–ultra vy. lt.
362	437	Tan–lt.
379	840	Beige Brown–med.
380	839	Beige Brown–dk.
397	762	Pearl Gray–vy. lt. (1 strand)
869	3743	Antique Violet–vy. lt. (1 strand)
397	762	Pearl Gray–vy. lt. (1 strand)
213	504	Blue Green–lt. (1 strand)
398	415	Pearl Gray (1 strand)
849	927	Slate Green–med. (1 strand)
398	415	Pearl Gray (1 strand)
875	503	Blue Green–med. (1 strand)
399	318	Steel Gray–lt. (1 strand)
121	793	Cornflower Blue–med. (1 strand)
399	318	Steel Gray–lt. (1 strand)
849	927	Slate Green–med. (1 strand)
399	318	Steel Gray–lt. (1 strand)
876	502	Blue Green (1 strand)

Step 2:   Backstitch (1 strand)

Anchor	DMC	Color
970	315	Antique Mauve–vy. dk.
871	3041	Antique Violet–med.
876	3740	Antique Violet–dk.
840	3768	Slate Green–dk.
379	840	Beige Brown–med.

Top

380 839 Beige Brown–dk.

Step 3:   French Knot (1 strand)

969 3727 Antique Mauve–lt.

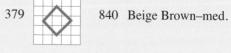

Step 4:   Long Stitch (1 strand)

379 840 Beige Brown–med.

Step 5:   Beadwork

02001 Pearl

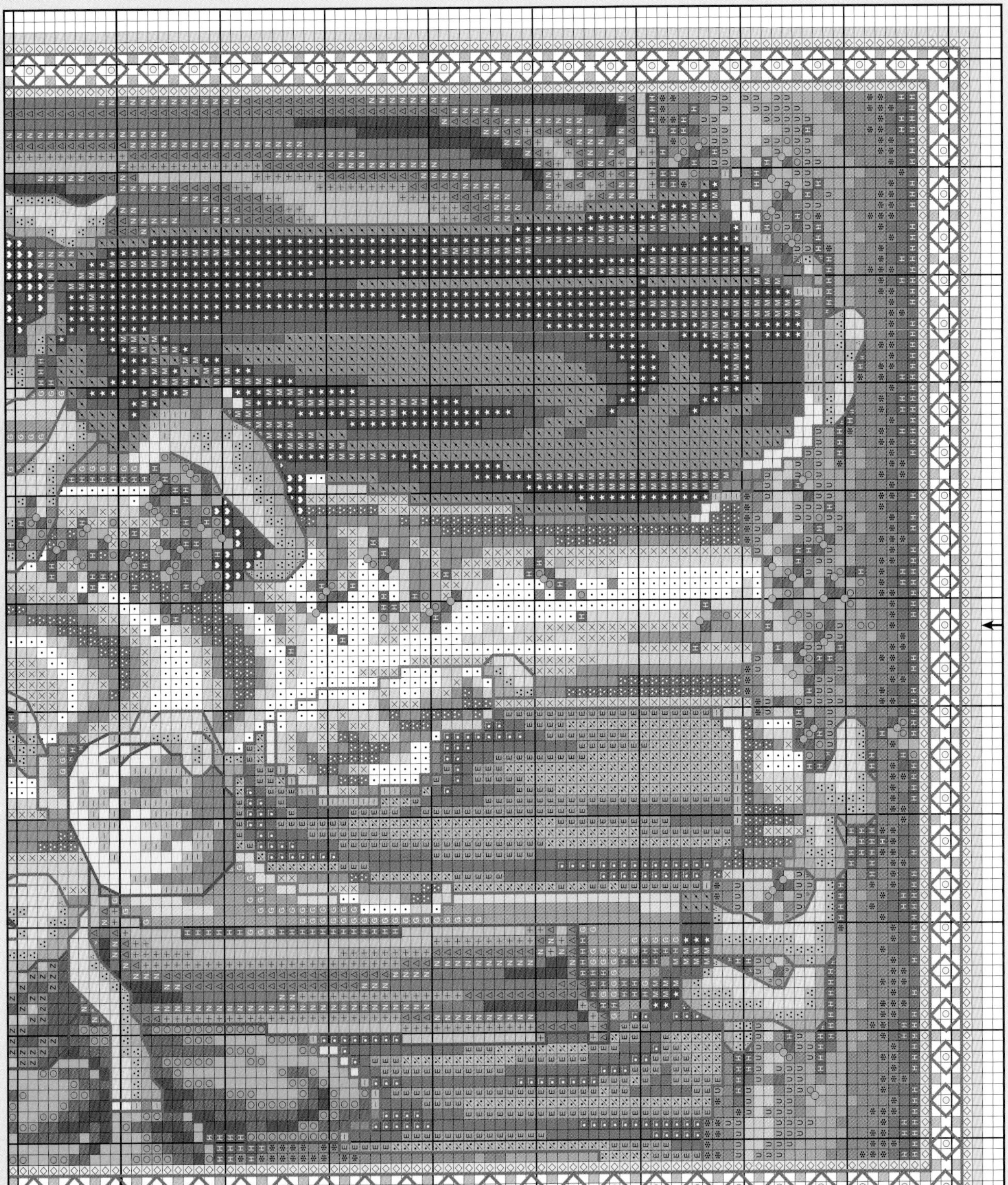

Bottom

Scenes of the Nativity

The samples were stitched on Vintage Linen 32 over 2. The finished design size for the left and right sections is 4¾" x 9½". The finished design size for the middle section is 6¼" x 12½". The fabric for the left and right sections was cut 11" x 17". The fabric for the middle section was cut 13" x 19".

Anchor   DMC

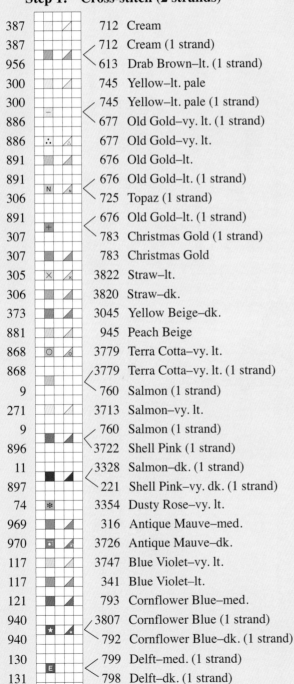

Step 1:   Cross-stitch (2 strands)

Anchor	DMC	
387	712	Cream
387	712	Cream (1 strand)
956	613	Drab Brown–lt. (1 strand)
300	745	Yellow–lt. pale
300	745	Yellow–lt. pale (1 strand)
886	677	Old Gold–vy. lt. (1 strand)
886	677	Old Gold–vy. lt.
891	676	Old Gold–lt.
891	676	Old Gold–lt. (1 strand)
306	725	Topaz (1 strand)
891	676	Old Gold–lt. (1 strand)
307	783	Christmas Gold (1 strand)
307	783	Christmas Gold
305	3822	Straw–lt.
306	3820	Straw–dk.
373	3045	Yellow Beige–dk.
881	945	Peach Beige
868	3779	Terra Cotta–vy. lt.
868	3779	Terra Cotta–vy. lt. (1 strand)
9	760	Salmon (1 strand)
271	3713	Salmon–vy. lt.
9	760	Salmon (1 strand)
896	3722	Shell Pink (1 strand)
11	3328	Salmon–dk. (1 strand)
897	221	Shell Pink–vy. dk. (1 strand)
74	3354	Dusty Rose–vy. lt.
969	316	Antique Mauve–med.
970	3726	Antique Mauve–dk.
117	3747	Blue Violet–vy. lt.
117	341	Blue Violet–lt.
121	793	Cornflower Blue–med.
940	3807	Cornflower Blue (1 strand)
940	792	Cornflower Blue–dk. (1 strand)
130	799	Delft–med. (1 strand)
131	798	Delft–dk. (1 strand)
132	797	Royal Blue
150	823	Navy Blue–dk.
214	966	Baby Green–med.
216	367	Pistachio Green–dk.
265	3348	Yellow Green–lt. (1 strand)
860	3053	Green Gray (1 strand)
843	3364	Pine Green
861	3363	Pine Green–med.
861	3363	Pine Green–med. (1 strand)
862	520	Fern Green–dk. (1 strand)
876	3816	Celadon Green
877	3815	Celadon Green–dk.
879	500	Blue Green–vy. dk.
851	924	Slate Green–vy. dk.
942	738	Tan–vy. lt.
362	437	Tan–lt. (1 strand)
886	677	Old Gold–vy. lt. (1 strand)
362	437	Tan–lt. (1 strand)
888	3828	Hazel Nut Brown (1 strand)
363	436	Tan
832	612	Drab Brown–med.
888	3828	Hazel Nut Brown (1 strand)
375	420	Hazel Nut Brown–dk. (1 strand)
375	420	Hazel Nut Brown–dk. (1 strand)
380	839	Beige Brown–dk. (1 strand)
8581	3023	Brown Gray–lt.
8581	3022	Brown Gray–med.
382	3021	Brown Gray–vy. dk.
905	645	Beaver Gray–vy. dk.
403	310	Black

Step 2:   Backstitch (1 strand)

Anchor	DMC	
387	712	Cream (2 strands)
305	3822	Straw–lt.
306	3820	Straw–dk.
306	3820	Straw–dk. (2 strands) (halo)
881	945	Peach Beige (2 strands)
896	3722	Shell Pink
11	3328	Salmon–dk.
74	3354	Dusty Rose–vy. lt.

Top of Middle Section

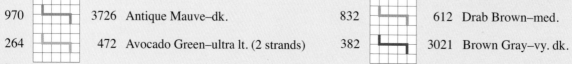

970   3726   Antique Mauve–dk.

264   472   Avocado Green–ultra lt. (2 strands)

832   612   Drab Brown–med.

382   3021   Brown Gray–vy. dk.

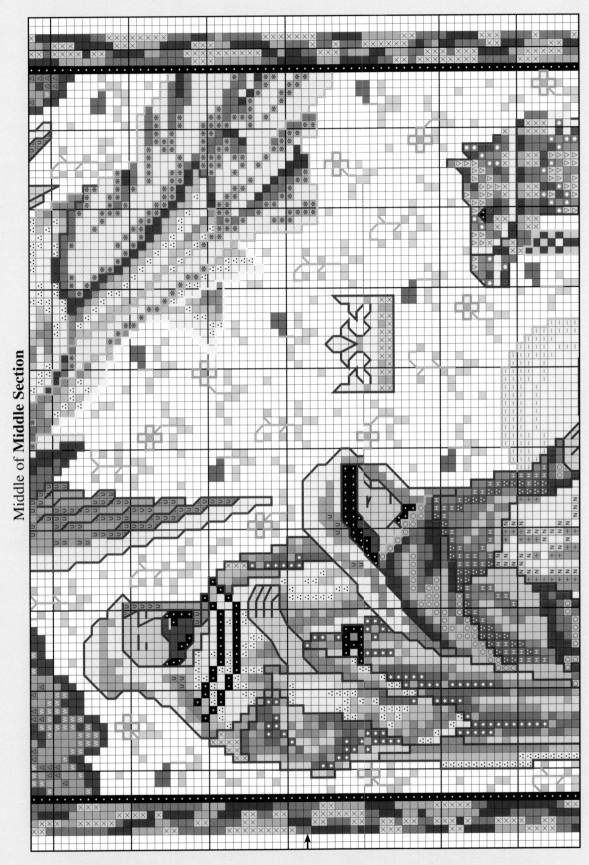

382   3021 Brown Gray–vy. dk. (2 strands) (eyes)

Step 3:   French Knot (1 strand)

11   3328 Salmon–dk.

Bottom of **Middle Section**

Bottom of **Left Section**

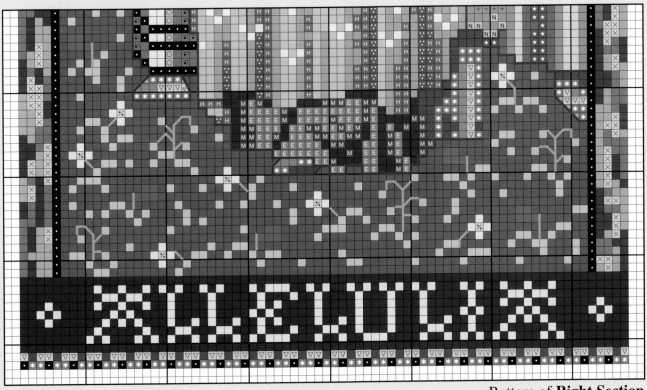

Bottom of **Right Section**

Last Supper

The sample was stitched on Light Mocha Cashel Linen 28 over 2. The finished design size is 17⅞" x 11⅝". The fabric was cut 24" x 18".

Anchor   DMC

Step 1:   Cross-stitch (2 strands)

Anchor	DMC	
387	712	Cream
387	712	Cream (1 strand)
891	676	Old Gold–lt. (1 strand)
387	712	Cream (1 strand)
942	738	Tan– vy. lt. (1 strand)
891	676	Old Gold–lt.
886	3047	Yellow Beige–lt.
887	3046	Yellow Beige–med.
373	3045	Yellow Beige–dk.
881	945	Peach Beige (1 strand)
882	3773	Pecan–vy. lt. (1 strand)
882	3773	Pecan–vy. lt.
892	819	Baby Pink–lt.
892	819	Baby Pink–lt. (1 strand)
25	3326	Rose–lt. (1 strand)
50	605	Cranberry–vy. lt.
50	605	Cranberry–vy. lt. (1 strand)
76	961	Wild Rose–dk. (1 strand)
25	3326	Rose–lt.
25	3326	Rose–lt. (1 strand)
894	223	Shell Pink–med. (1 strand)
76	961	Wild Rose–dk.
42	3350	Dusty Rose–dk.
894	223	Shell Pink–med.
896	3722	Shell Pink
78	3803	Mauve–dk.
1019	3802	Antique Mauve–deep
99	552	Violet–dk.
99	552	Violet–dk. (1 strand)
101	550	Violet–vy. dk. (1 strand)
101	550	Violet–vy.dk.
872	3740	Antique Violet–dk.
872	3740	Antique Violet–dk. (1 strand)
119	333	Blue Violet–vy. dk. (1 strand)
117	341	Blue Violet–lt.
118	340	Blue Violet–med.
118	340	Blue Violet–med. (1 strand)
119	333	Blue Violet–vy. dk. (1 strand)
130	809	Delft

Anchor	DMC	
130	799	Delft–med.
131	798	Delft–dk.
132	797	Royal Blue
134	820	Royal Blue–vy. dk.
121	793	Cornflower Blue–med.
940	792	Cornflower Blue–dk.
940	792	Cornflower Blue–dk. (1 strand)
941	791	Cornflower Blue–vy. dk. (1 strand)
941	791	Cornflower Blue–vy. dk.
941	791	Cornflower Blue–vy. dk. (1 strand)
845	3011	Khaki Green–dk. (1 strand)
842	3013	Khaki Green–lt.
844	3012	Khaki Green–med.
845	3011	Khaki Green–dk.
874	834	Olive Green–vy. lt.
874	833	Olive Green–lt.
889	831	Olive Green–med.
942	738	Tan–vy. lt.
942	738	Tan–vy. lt. (1 strand)
363	436	Tan (1 strand)
363	436	Tan
370	434	Brown–lt.
371	433	Brown–med.
380	839	Beige Brown–dk.
397	453	Shell Gray–lt.
397	453	Shell Gray–lt. (1 strand)
399	451	Dhell Gray–dk. (1 strand)
399	451	Shell Gray–dk.
401	535	Ash Gray–vy. lt.

Step 2:   Backstitch (1 strand)

Anchor	DMC	
881	945	Peach Beige (2 strands)
1019	3802	Antique Mauve–deep (2 strands)
872	3740	Antique Violet–dk.
380	839	Beige Brown–dk.
380	839	Beige Brown–dk. (2 strands)
401	535	Ash Gray–vy. lt.

Step 3:   Long Stitch (1 strand)

Anchor	DMC	
387	712	Cream
891	676	Old Gold–lt.
380	839	Beige Brown–dk.
401	535	Ash Gray–vy. lt. (2 strands)

Stitch Count: 250 width x 162 length

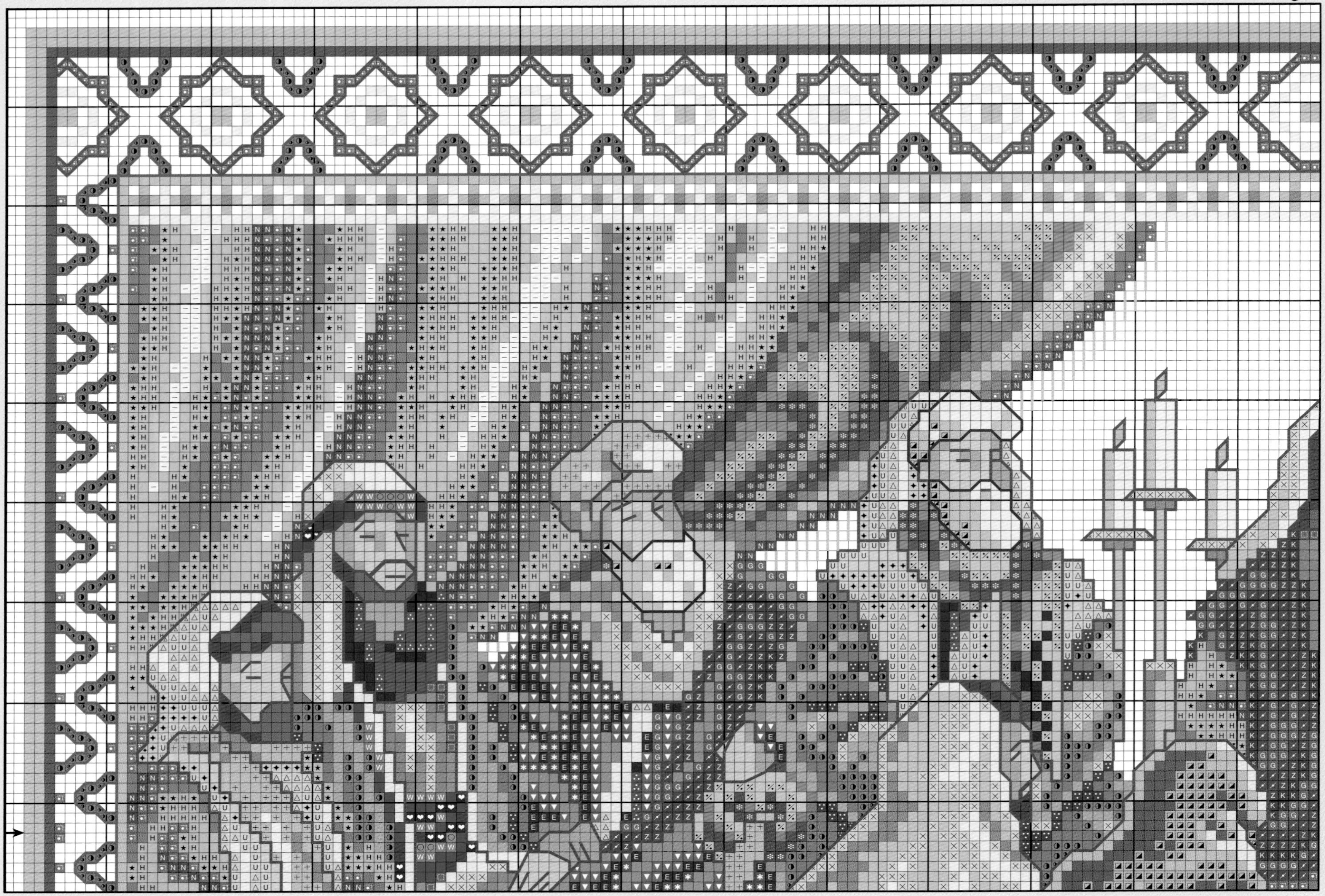

Top Right

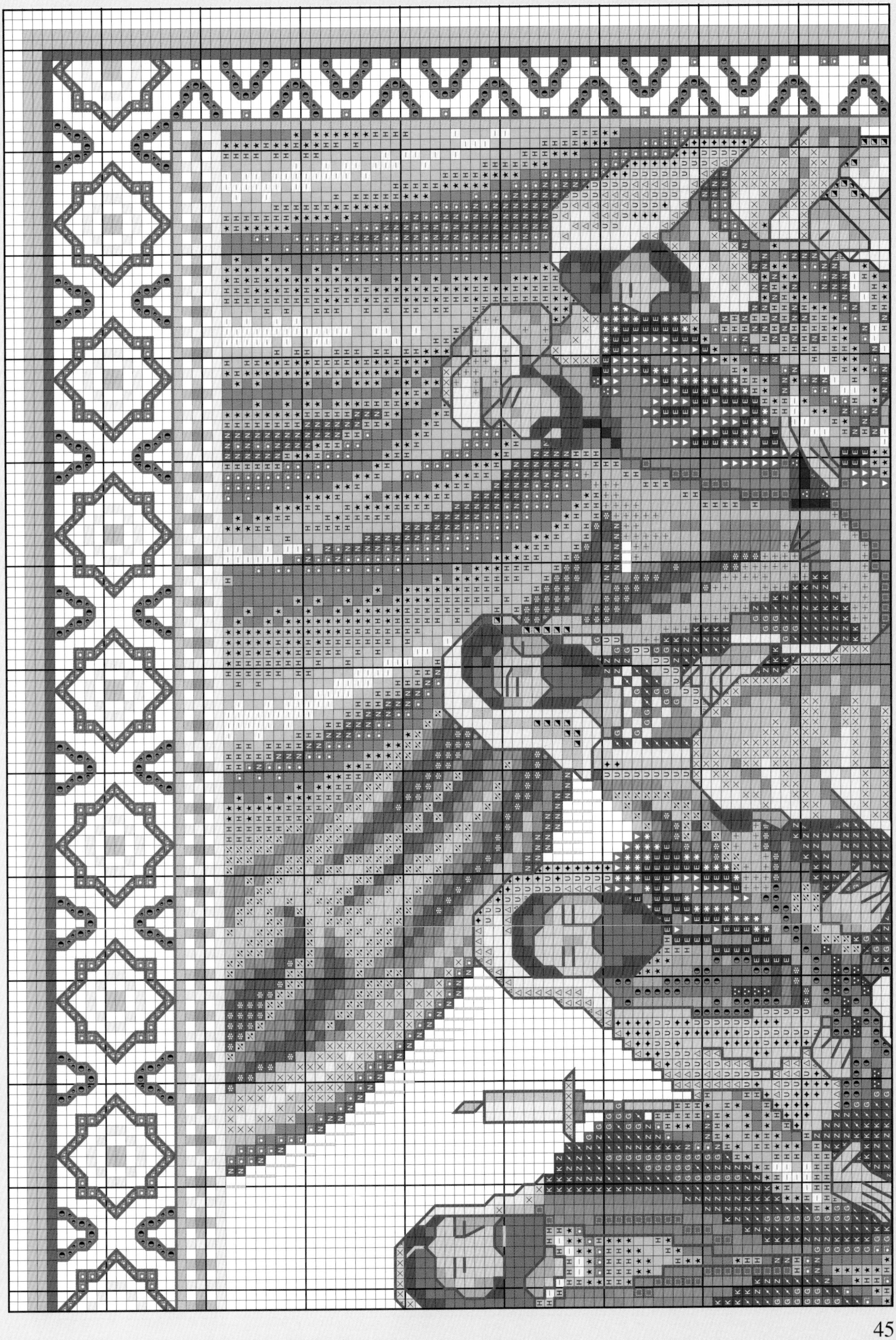

Bottom Left

The Lion & the Lamb

The sample was stitched on Cobblestone Cashel Linen 28 over 2. The finished design size is 12⅛" x 7⅞". The fabric was cut 19" x 14".

Anchor   **DMC**

Step 1:   Cross-stitch (2 strands)

Anchor		DMC	
926			Ecru
886		677	Old Gold–vy. lt.
886		677	Old Gold–vy. lt. (1 strand)
907		3821	Straw (1 strand)
891		676	Old Gold–lt.
890		729	Old Gold–med.
890		729	Old Gold–med. (1 strand)
308		976	Golden Brown–med. (1 strand)
309		782	Topaz–med. (1 strand)
375		420	Hazel Nut Brown–dk. (1 strand)
305		3822	Straw–lt.
306		3820	Straw–dk.
8		353	Peach
9		760	Salmon (1 strand)
10		3712	Salmon–med. (1 strand)
11		3328	Salmon–dk. (1 strand)
897		221	Shell Pink–vy. dk. (1 strand)
75		3733	Dusty Rose–lt.
87		3607	Plum–lt. (1 strand)
69		3687	Mauve (1 strand)
78		3803	Mauve–med.
1019		3802	Antique Mauve–deep (1 strand)
403		310	Black (1 strand)
101		550	Violet–vy. dk. (1 strand)
905		3781	Mocha Brown–dk. (1 strand)
120		794	Cornflower Blue–lt.
121		793	Cornflower Blue–med. (1 strand)
122		3807	Cornflower Blue (1 strand)
940		792	Cornflower Blue–dk.
941		791	Cornflower Blue–vy. dk.
264		472	Avocado Green–ultra lt.
266		471	Avocado Green–vy. lt. (1 strand)
257		3346	Hunter Green (1 strand)
242		989	Forest Green (1 strand)
214		368	Pistachio Green–lt. (1 strand)
214		368	Pistachio Green–lt.
216		367	Pistachio Green–dk. (1 strand)
212		561	Jade–vy. dk. (1 strand)
877		3815	Celadon Green–dk.
877		3815	Celadon Green–dk. (1 strand)
905		3781	Mocha Brown–dk. (1 strand)
862		3362	Pine Green–dk.
879		500	Blue Green–vy. dk. (1 strand)
862		934	Black Avocado Green (1 strand)
888		3828	Hazel Nut Brown
371		433	Brown–med.
357		801	Coffee Brown–dk.
903		640	Beige Gray–vy. dk.
8581		3023	Brown Gray–lt.
273		3787	Brown Gray–dk.
403		310	Black

Step 2:   Backstitch (1 strand)

Anchor		DMC	
905		3781	Mocha Brown–dk.
403		310	Black (2 strands)
403		310	Black

Step 3:   French Knot (1 strand)

Anchor		DMC	
926			Ecru
905		3781	Mocha Brown–dk.

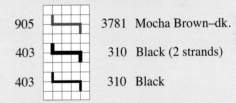

Noah's Ark

The sample was stitched on Driftwood Dublin Linen 25 over 2. The finished design size is 9⅝" x 8⅜". The fabric was cut 16" x 15".

Anchor   **DMC**

Step 1:   Cross-stitch (2 strands)

Anchor		DMC	
1			White
387		712	Cream
293		727	Topaz–vy. lt.
295		726	Topaz–lt. (1 strand)
307		977	Golden Brown–lt. (1 strand)
300		745	Yellow–lt. pale
886		677	Old Gold–vy. lt.
891		676	Old Gold–lt. (1 strand)
890		729	Old Gold–med. (1 strand)
300		745	Yellow–lt. pale (1 strand)
295		726	Topaz–lt. (1 strand)
295		726	Topaz–lt. (1 strand)
307		783	Christmas Gold (1 strand)
307		783	Christmas Gold
11		351	Coral
968		778	Antique Mauve–vy. lt.
108		211	Lavender–lt. (1 strand)
117		3747	Blue Violet–vy. lt. (1 strand)
975		3753	Antique Blue–ultra vy. lt.
920		932	Antique Blue–lt.
121		793	Cornflower Blue–med. (1 strand)
119		333	Blue Violet–vy. dk. (1 strand)
187		958	Seagreen–dk. (1 strand)
1039		3810	Turquoise–dk. (1 strand)
858		524	Fern Green–vy. lt.
859		3052	Green Gray–med.
846		3051	Green Gray–dk.
347		402	Mahogany–vy. lt. (1 strand)
308		976	Golden Brown–med. (1 strand)

Anchor		DMC	
355		3826	Golden Brown
370		434	Brown–lt. (1 strand)
382		3021	Brown Gray–vy. dk. (1 strand)
373		422	Hazel Nut Brown–lt.
375		420	Hazel Nut Brown–dk.
375		420	Hazel Nut Brown–dk. (1 strand)
970		315	Antique Mauve–vy. dk. (1 strand)
375		420	Hazel Nut Brown–dk. (1 strand)
307		977	Golden Brown–lt. (1 strand)
375		420	Hazel Nut Brown–dk. (1 strand)
889		610	Drab Brown–vy. dk. (1 strand)
832		612	Drab Brown–med. (1 strand)
898		611	Drab Brown–dk. (1 strand)
898		611	Drab Brown–dk. (1 strand)
888		3828	Hazel Nut Brown–med. (1 strand)
889		610	Drab Brown–vy. dk. (1 strand)
401		844	Beaver Gray–ultra dk. (1 strand)
900		3024	Brown Gray–vy. lt.
382		3021	Brown Gray–vy. dk.
8581		647	Beaver Gray–med.
905		645	Beaver Gray–vy. dk.
401		844	Beaver Gray–ultra dk.
403		310	Black

Step 2:   Backstitch (1 strand)

Anchor		DMC	
355		3826	Golden Brown
382		3021	Brown Gray–vy. dk.
403		310	Black

Step 3:   French Knot (1 strand)

Anchor		DMC	
387		712	Cream
888		3828	Hazel Nut Brown–med.
382		3021	Brown Gray–vy. dk.

Christmas Play

The sample was stitched on Cameo Rose Cashel Linen 28 over 2. The finished design size is 8⅝" x 7⅞". The fabric was cut 15" x 14".

Anchor　　**DMC**

Step 1:　Cross Stitch (2 strands)

Anchor		DMC	
1			White
387		712	Cream
300		745	Yellow–lt. pale
891		676	Old Gold–lt. (1 strand)
881		945	Peach Beige (1 strand)
891		676	Old Gold–lt.
881		945	Peach Beige
10		3712	Salmon–med.
86		3608	Plum–vy. lt.
104		210	Lavender–med.
101		327	Antique Violet–vy. dk.
119		333	Blue Violet–vy. dk.
117		3747	Blue Violet–vy. lt.
145		334	Baby Blue–med.
978		322	Navy Blue–vy. lt.
121		793	Cornflower Blue–med.
858		524	Fern Green–vy. lt.
860		3053	Green Gray
363		436	Tan
375		420	Hazel Nut Brown–dk.
900		3024	Brown Gray–vy. lt.
382		3021	Brown Gray–vy. dk.

Step 2:　Backstitch (2 strands)

Anchor		DMC	
1			White
387		712	Cream
300		745	Yellow–lt. pale
891		676	Old Gold–lt.
101		327	Antique Violet–vy. dk.
119		333	Blue Violet–vy. dk.
121		793	Cornflower Blue–med.
382		3021	Brown Gray–vy. dk. (1 strand)

59

A Good Report

The sample was stitched on Platinum Cashel Linen 28 over 2. The finished design size is 5⅛" x 6⅝". The fabric was cut 12" x 13".

Anchor　　**DMC**

Step 1:　Cross-stitch (2 strands)

Anchor	DMC	
1		White
886	677	Old Gold–vy. lt.
891	676	Old Gold–lt.
306	725	Topaz
366	951	Peach Pecan–lt.
4146	950	Peach Pecan–dk.
11	351	Coral
1014	3830	Terra Cotta–dk.
95	554	Violet–lt.
154	3755	Baby Blue
842	3013	Khaki Green–lt.
373	422	Hazel Nut Brown–lt.

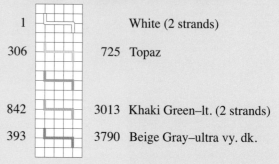

Anchor	DMC	
363	436	Tan
388	3033	Mocha Brown–vy. lt.
888	3828	Hazel Nut Brown (1 strand)
379	840	Beige Brown–med. (1 strand)
393	3790	Beige Gray–ultra vy. dk.
900	648	Beaver Gray–lt.
878	501	Blue Green–dk. (1 strand)
401	535	Ash Gray–vy. lt. (1 strand)

Step 2:　Backstitch (1 strand)

Anchor	DMC	
1		White (2 strands)
306	725	Topaz
842	3013	Khaki Green–lt. (2 strands)
393	3790	Beige Gray–ultra vy. dk.

A Praying Child

The sample was stitched on Rose Lugana 25 over 2. The finished design size is 5¾" x 7⅜". The fabric was cut 11" x 14".

Anchor　　**DMC**

Step 1:　Cross-stitch (2 strands)

Anchor	DMC	
1		White
886	677	Old Gold–vy. lt.
891	676	Old Gold–lt.
881	945	Peach Beige
881	945	Peach Beige (1 strand)
882	3773	Pecan–vy. lt. (1 strand)
49	963	Wild Rose–vy. lt.
74	3354	Dusty Rose–vy. lt.
66	3688	Mauve–med.
69	3687	Mauve
969	316	Antique Mauve–med.
78	3803	Mauve–dk.

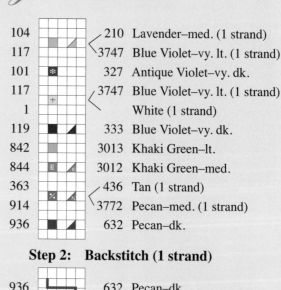

Anchor	DMC	
104	210	Lavender–med. (1 strand)
117	3747	Blue Violet–vy. lt. (1 strand)
101	327	Antique Violet–vy. dk.
117	3747	Blue Violet–vy. lt. (1 strand)
1		White (1 strand)
119	333	Blue Violet–vy. dk.
842	3013	Khaki Green–lt.
844	3012	Khaki Green–med.
363	436	Tan (1 strand)
914	3772	Pecan–med. (1 strand)
936	632	Pecan–dk.

Step 2:　Backstitch (1 strand)

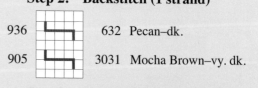

Anchor	DMC	
936	632	Pecan–dk.
905	3031	Mocha Brown–vy. dk.

Step 3:　French Knot (1 strand)

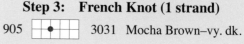

Anchor	DMC	
905	3031	Mocha Brown–vy. dk.

Scripture Reading (see code page 66) – Stitch Count: 72 width x 92 length

Scripture Reading

The sample was stitched on Periwinkle Pastel Linen 28 over 2. The finished design size is 5⅛" x 6⅝". The fabric was cut 12" x 13".

Anchor	DMC	

Step 1: Cross-stitch (2 strands)

Anchor		DMC	
1			White
300		3823	Yellow–ultra pale
301		745	Yellow–pale
891		676	Old Gold–lt.
373		3045	Yellow Beige–dk.
366		951	Peach Pecan–lt.
4146		950	Peach Pecan–dk.
893		224	Shell Pink–lt.
894		223	Shell Pink–med.
970		3726	Antique Mauve–dk.
871		3041	Antique Violet–med. (1 strand)
373		3045	Yellow Beige–dk. (1 strand)
128		800	Delft–pale
159		827	Blue–vy. lt. (1 strand)
160		813	Blue–lt. (1 strand)
161		826	Blue–med.
162		825	Blue–dk.
164		824	Blue–vy. dk.
264		472	Avocado Green–ultra lt.
267		470	Avocado Green–lt.
843		3364	Pine Green
861		3363	Pine Green–med.
862		3362	Pine Green–dk. (1 strand)
267		470	Avocado Green–lt. (1 strand)
874		834	Olive Green–vy. lt.
388		3033	Mocha Brown–vy. lt.
363		436	Tan
309		435	Brown–vy. lt.
900		648	Beaver Gray–lt.
8581		647	Beaver Gray–med.
403		310	Black

Step 2: Backstitch (1 strand)

Anchor		DMC	
393		3790	Beige Gray–ultra vy. dk.
403		310	Black

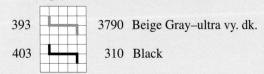

Santa

See photo, page 69. The sample was stitched on Blue Wing Linen 28 over 2. The finished design size is 8⅝" x 7⅞". The fabric was cut 15" x 14".

Anchor	DMC	

Step 1: Cross-stitch (2 strands)

Anchor		DMC	
1			White
300		3823	Yellow–ultra pale
301		745	Yellow–lt. pale (1 strand)
306		725	Topaz (1 strand)
306		725	Topaz (1 strand)
307		783	Christmas Gold (1 strand)
307		783	Christmas Gold (1 strand)
944		869	Hazel Nut Brown–vy. dk. (1 strand)
4146		754	Peach–lt.
4146		754	Peach–lt. (1 strand)
914		3064	Pecan–lt. (1 strand)
4146		754	Peach–lt. (1 strand)
9		760	Salmon (1 strand)
13		347	Salmon–vy. dk.
47		304	Christmas Red–med.
43		815	Garnet–med.
72		902	Garnet–vy. dk.
104		210	Lavender–med. (1 strand)
105		209	Lavender–dk. (1 strand)
110		208	Lavender–vy. dk.
101		327	Antique Violet–vy. dk.
117		3747	Blue Violet–vy. lt.
117		3747	Blue Violet–vy. lt. (1 strand)
121		793	Cornflower Blue–med. (1 strand)
940		3807	Cornflower Blue
940		792	Cornflower Blue–dk. (1 strand)
101		327	Antique Violet–vy. dk. (1 strand)
158		775	Baby Blue–vy. lt.
158		775	Baby Blue–vy. lt. (1 strand)
094			Star Blue BF (2 strands)
343		3752	Antique Blue–vy. lt.
343		3752	Antique Blue–vy. lt. (1 strand)
094			Star Blue BF (2 strands)
920		932	Antique Blue–lt.
920		932	Antique Blue–lt. (1 strand)
094			Star Blue BF (2 strands)
921		931	Antique Blue–med. (1 strand)
400		414	Steel Gray–dk. (1 strand)

214			368	Pistachio Green–lt. (1 strand)
877			3815	Celadon Green–dk. (1 strand)
212			561	Jade–vy. dk.
879			500	Blue Green–vy. dk.
944			869	Hazel Nut Brown–vy. dk.
397			3072	Beaver Gray–vy. lt.
900			648	Beaver Gray–lt.
8581			647	Beaver Gray–med.
403			310	Black

Step 2: Backstitch (1 strand)

1		White
	032	Pearl Very Fine Braid
	102	Vatican Gold Very Fine Braid
920	932	Antique Blue–lt. (1 strand)
	094	Star Blue BF (1 strand)
944	869	Hazel Nut Brown–vy. dk.
400	414	Steel Gray–dk.
403	310	Black

Step 3: French Knot (1 strand)

| 43 | | 815 | Garnet–med. |

Step 4: Long Stitch (1 strand)

| | 032 | Pearl Very Fine Braid |

Step 5: Stars (1 strand)

1		White
	032	Pearl Very Fine Braid
	102	Vatican Gold Very Fine Braid

Step 6: Wrapped Backstitch

| 301 | | 745 | Yellow–lt. pale (1 strand) |
| | | | (wrap with 002 Gold BF 2 strands) |

Step 7: Beadwork

| | | 00479 | White |

Santa – Stitch Count: 120 width x 110 length

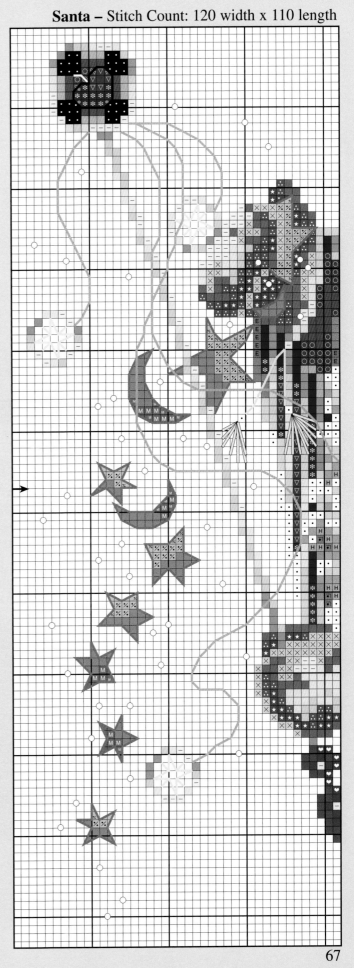

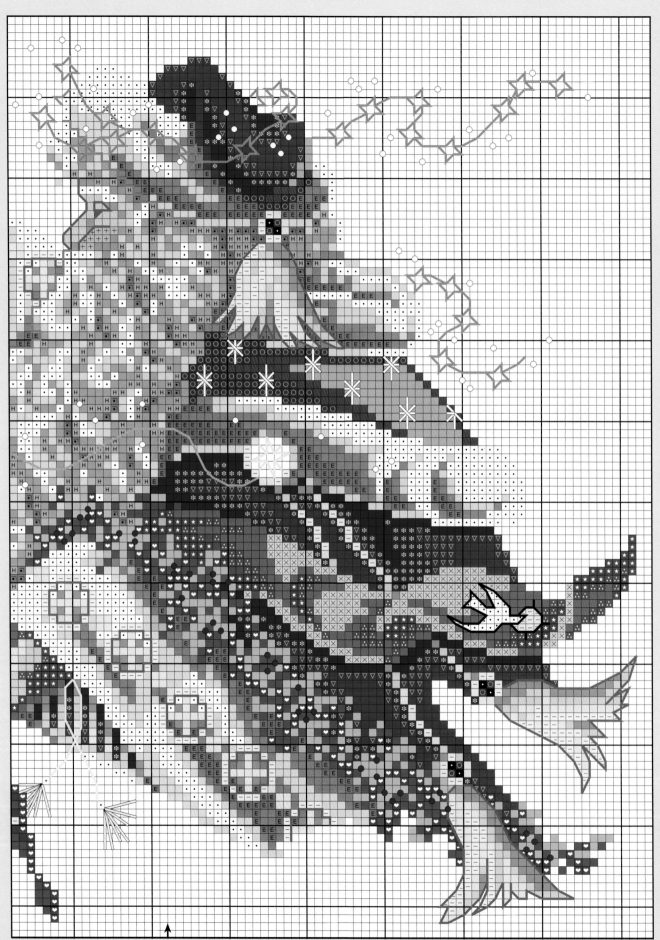

Kids Count

The sample was stitched on Toasted Almond Cashel Linen 28 over 2. The finished design size is 12⅛" x 6⅛". The fabric was cut 19" x 13".

Anchor	DMC	

Step 1: Cross-stitch (2 strands)

Anchor	DMC	
1		White
1		White (1 strand)
891	676	Old Gold–lt. (1 strand)
300	745	Yellow–lt. pale
891	676	Old Gold–lt. (1 strand)
306	3820	Straw–dk. (1 strand)
308	782	Topaz–med.
366	951	Peach Pecan–lt.
881	945	Peach Beige
49	963	Wild Rose–vy. lt. (1 strand)
75	604	Cranberry–lt. (1 strand)
75	604	Cranberry–lt. (1 strand)
69	3687	Mauve (1 strand)
69	3687	Mauve (1 strand)
341	3777	Terra Cotta–vy. dk. (1 strand)
896	3722	Shell Pink
44	814	Garnet–dk.
86	3608	Plum–vy. lt.
87	3607	Plum–lt.
78	3803	Mauve–med.
95	554	Violet–lt.
110	208	Lavender–vy. dk.
110	208	Lavender–vy. dk. (1 strand)
940	792	Cornflower Blue–dk. (1 strand)
101	327	Antique Violet–vy. dk.
117	3747	Blue Violet–vy. lt.
117	341	Blue Violet–lt. (1 strand)
118	340	Blue Violet–med. (1 strand)
121	793	Cornflower Blue–med.
940	792	Cornflower Blue–dk.
150	823	Navy Blue–dk.
921	931	Antique Blue–med.
860	3053	Green Gray (1 strand)
266	581	Moss Green (1 strand)
859	3052	Gren Gray–med. (1 strand)
268	937	Avocado Green–med. (1 strand)
379	890	Pistachio Green–ultra dk. (1 strand)
382	3371	Black Brown (1 strand)
311	3827	Golden Brown–pale
307	977	Golden Brown–lt. (1 strand)
888	3828	Hazel Nut Brown (1 strand)
942	738	Tan–vy. lt.
888	3828	Hazel Nut Brown
888	3828	Hazel Nut Brown (1 strand)
370	434	Brown–lt. (1 strand)
944	869	Hazel Nut Brown–vy. dk.
379	840	Beige Brown–med.
380	839	Beige Brown–dk.
360	898	Coffee Brown–vy. dk.
101	327	Antique Violet–vy. dk. (1 strand)
382	3371	Black Brown (1 strand)
8581	646	Beaver Gray–dk.
236	3799	Pewter Gray–vy. dk.

Step 2: Backstitch (1 strand)

Anchor	DMC	
1		White
101	327	Antique Violet–vy. dk.
360	898	Coffee Brown–vy. dk.
382	3371	Black Brown

Step 3: French Knot (1 strand)

Anchor	DMC	
360	898	Coffee Brown–vy. dk.
382	3371	Black Brown

Two by Two

The sample was stitched on Antique White Cashel Linen 28 over 2. The finished design size is 7⅞" x 10¾". The fabric was cut 14" x 17".

Anchor   DMC

Step 1:   Cross-stitch (2 strands)

Anchor	DMC	
1		White
891	676	Old Gold–lt.
307	783	Christmas Gold
868	758	Terra Cotta–lt.
5975	356	Terra Cotta–med.
49	963	Wild Rose–vy. lt.
50	605	Cranberry–vy. lt.
46	666	Christmas Red–bright
897	221	Shell Pink–dk.
22	816	Garnet
871	3041	Antique Violet–med.
167	519	Sky Blue
132	797	Royal Blue
185	964	Seagreen–lt.
186	959	Seagreen–med.
188	3812	Seagreen–vy. dk.
206	955	Nile Green–lt.
204	912	Emerald Green–lt.
205	911	Emerald Green–med.
203	564	Jade–vy. lt.

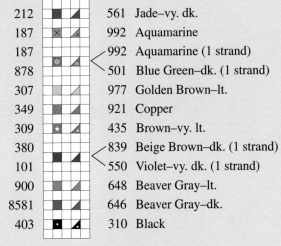

Anchor	DMC	
212	561	Jade–vy. dk.
187	992	Aquamarine
187	992	Aquamarine (1 strand)
878	501	Blue Green–dk. (1 strand)
307	977	Golden Brown–lt.
349	921	Copper
309	435	Brown–vy. lt.
380	839	Beige Brown–dk. (1 strand)
101	550	Violet–vy. dk. (1 strand)
900	648	Beaver Gray–lt.
8581	646	Beaver Gray–dk.
403	310	Black

Step 2:   Backstitch (1 strand)

Anchor	DMC	
307	783	Christmas Gold (2 strands)
101	550	Violet–vy. dk.
380	839	Beige Brown–dk.

Step 3:   French Knot (1 strand)

Anchor	DMC	
1		White
307	783	Christmas Gold
380	839	Beige Brown–dk.

Step 4:   Long Stitch (1 strand)

Anchor	DMC	
307	783	Christmas Gold

Top

Bottom

Animal Angels

Puppy Angel

The sample was stitched on Star Sapphire Linen 28 over 2. The finished design size is 5⅜" x 5⅜". The fabric was cut 12" x 12".

Anchor   DMC

Step 1:   Cross-stitch (2 strands)

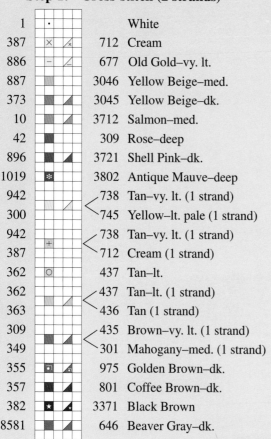

Anchor	DMC	
1		White
387	712	Cream
886	677	Old Gold–vy. lt.
887	3046	Yellow Beige–med.
373	3045	Yellow Beige–dk.
10	3712	Salmon–med.
42	309	Rose–deep
896	3721	Shell Pink–dk.
1019	3802	Antique Mauve–deep
942	738	Tan–vy. lt. (1 strand)
300	745	Yellow–lt. pale (1 strand)
942	738	Tan–vy. lt. (1 strand)
387	712	Cream (1 strand)
362	437	Tan–lt.
362	437	Tan–lt. (1 strand)
363	436	Tan (1 strand)
309	435	Brown–vy. lt. (1 strand)
349	301	Mahogany–med. (1 strand)
355	975	Golden Brown–dk.
357	801	Coffee Brown–dk.
382	3371	Black Brown
8581	646	Beaver Gray–dk.

Step 2:   Backstitch (1 strand)

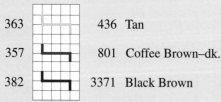

Anchor	DMC	
363	436	Tan
357	801	Coffee Brown–dk.
382	3371	Black Brown

Step 3:   French Knot (1 strand)

Anchor	DMC	
387	712	Cream

Squirrel Angel

The sample was stitched on Potato Annabelle 28 over 2. The finished design size is 4¾" x 5⅝". The fabric was cut 11" x 12".

Anchor   DMC

Step 1:   Cross-stitch (2 strands)

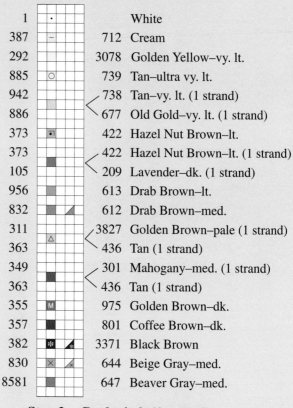

Anchor	DMC	
1		White
387	712	Cream
292	3078	Golden Yellow–vy. lt.
885	739	Tan–ultra vy. lt.
942	738	Tan–vy. lt. (1 strand)
886	677	Old Gold–vy. lt. (1 strand)
373	422	Hazel Nut Brown–lt.
373	422	Hazel Nut Brown–lt. (1 strand)
105	209	Lavender–dk. (1 strand)
956	613	Drab Brown–lt.
832	612	Drab Brown–med.
311	3827	Golden Brown–pale (1 strand)
363	436	Tan (1 strand)
349	301	Mahogany–med. (1 strand)
363	436	Tan (1 strand)
355	975	Golden Brown–dk.
357	801	Coffee Brown–dk.
382	3371	Black Brown
830	644	Beige Gray–med.
8581	647	Beaver Gray–med.

Step 2:   Backstitch (1 strand)

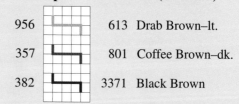

Anchor	DMC	
956	613	Drab Brown–lt.
357	801	Coffee Brown–dk.
382	3371	Black Brown

Step 3:   French Knot (1 strand)

Anchor	DMC	
1		White

Step 4:   Long Stitch (2 strands)

Anchor	DMC	
382	3371	Black Brown

Bear Angel

The sample was stitched on Cameo Rose Cashel Linen 28 over 2. The finished design size is 5¾" x 5⅞". The fabric was cut 12" x 12".

Anchor   DMC

Step 1:   Cross-stitch (2 strands)

Anchor		DMC	
1			White
387		712	Cream
886		677	Old Gold–vy. lt.
301		744	Yellow–pale
887		3046	Yellow Beige–med.
373		3045	Yellow Beige–dk.
366		951	Peach Pecan–lt.
49		3689	Mauve–lt.
66		3688	Mauve–med.
970		3726	Antique Mauve–dk.
869		3743	Antique Violet–vy. lt.
311		3827	Golden Brown–pale
307		977	Golden Brown–lt.
308		3826	Golden Brown
375		420	Hazel Nut Brown–dk.
379		840	Beige Brown–med.
942		738	Tan–vy. lt.
363		436	Tan
309		435	Brown–vy. lt.
371		433	Brown–med.
382		3371	Black Brown

Step 2:   Backstitch (1 strand)

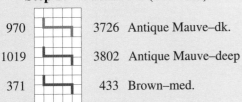

Anchor	DMC	
970	3726	Antique Mauve–dk.
1019	3802	Antique Mauve–deep
371	433	Brown–med.

Step 3:   French Knot (1 strand)

Anchor	DMC	
387	712	Cream
66	3688	Mauve–med.
382	3371	Black Brown

Bunny Angel

The sample was stitched on Antique Blue Linen 28 over 2. The finished design size is 5¼" x 6". The fabric was cut 12" x 12".

Anchor   DMC

Step 1:   Cross-stitch (2 strands)

Anchor		DMC	
1			White
387		712	Cream
886		677	Old Gold–vy. lt.
887		3046	Yellow Beige–med.
373		3045	Yellow Beige–dk.
366		951	Peach Pecan–lt.
8		761	Salmon–lt.
75		962	Wild Rose–med. (1 strand)
76		3731	Dusty Rose–med. (1 strand)
42		309	Rose–deep
373		422	Hazel Nut Brown–lt.
375		420	Hazel Nut Brown–dk.
942		738	Tan–vy. lt.
363		436	Tan
371		433	Brown–med.
381		938	Coffee Brown–ultra dk.
382		3371	Black Brown

Step 2:   Backstitch (1 strand)

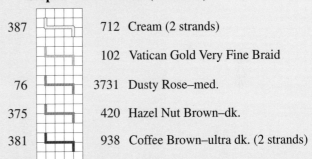

Anchor	DMC	
387	712	Cream (2 strands)
	102	Vatican Gold Very Fine Braid
76	3731	Dusty Rose–med.
375	420	Hazel Nut Brown–dk.
381	938	Coffee Brown–ultra dk. (2 strands)

Step 3:   French Knot (1 strand)

Anchor	DMC	
1		White

Step 4:   Long Stitch (1 strand)

Anchor	DMC	
387	712	Cream

Bear Angel – Stitch Count: 80 width x 82 length

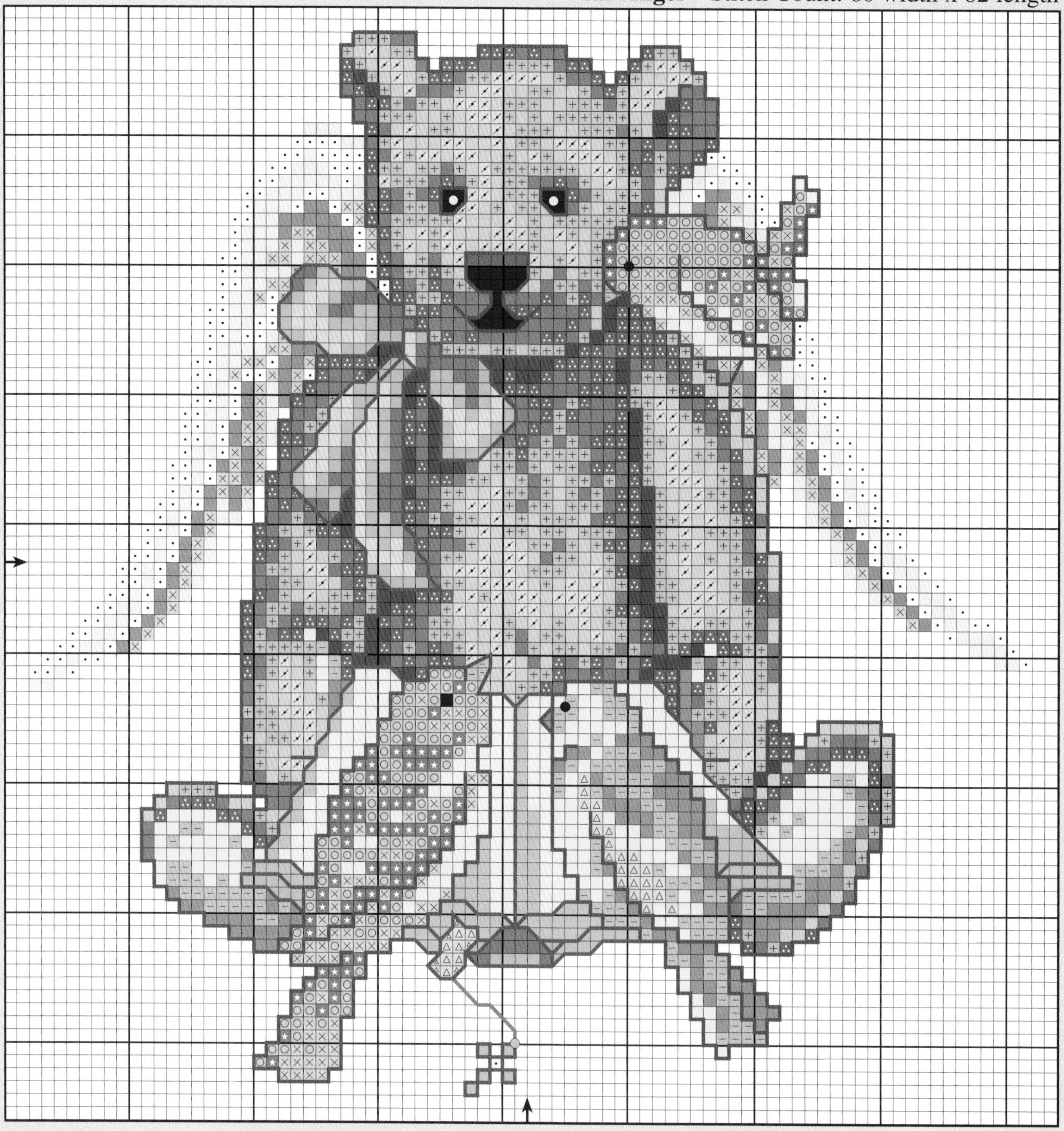

Kitten Angel – Stitch Count: 80 width x 70 length

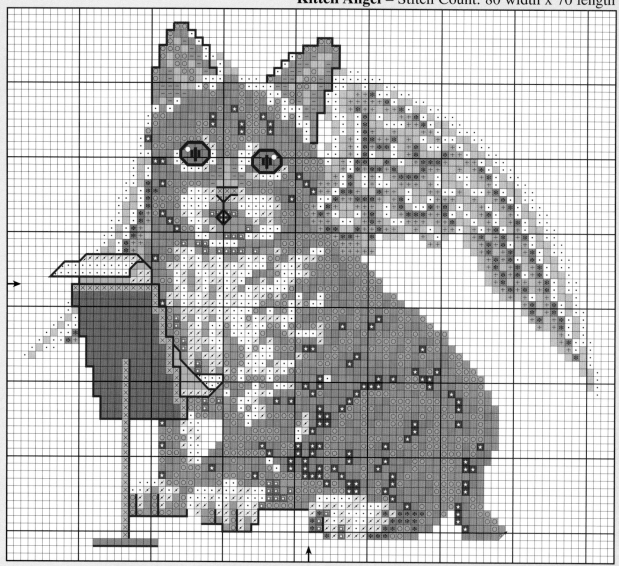

Kitten Angel

The sample was stitched on Lavender Mist Cashel Linen 28 over 2. The finished design size is 5¾" x 5". The fabric was cut 12" x 12".

Anchor   **DMC**

Step 1: Cross-stitch (2 strands)

Anchor		DMC	
1			White
868		3779	Terra Cotta–vy. lt.
337		3778	Terra Cotta
9		760	Salmon
896		3722	Shell Pink
158		3756	Baby Blue–ultra vy. lt.
159		3325	Baby Blue–lt.
779		926	Slate Green
885		739	Tan–ultra vy. lt. (1 strand)
956		613	Drab Brown–lt. (1 strand)

Anchor		DMC	
832		612	Drab Brown–med.
388		3033	Mocha Brown–vy. lt.
905		3031	Mocha Brown–vy. dk.
393		3790	Beige Gray–ultra vy. dk.
830		644	Beige Gray–med.
8581		647	Beaver Gray–med.
398		415	Pearl Gray
399		318	Steel Gray–lt.

Step 2: Backstitch (1 strand)

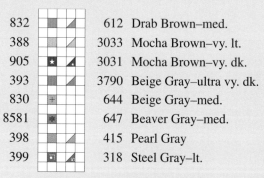

382		3371	Black Brown (2 strands) (eyes)
382		3371	Black Brown

Step 3: French Knot (1 strand)

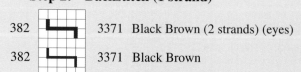

1			White

The sample was stitched on Periwinkle Pastel Linen 28 over 2. The finished design size is 4¼" x 5". The fabric was cut 11" x 11".

Anchor　　**DMC**

Step 1:　Cross-stitch (2 strands)

1		White
300		745	Yellow–lt. pale
886		677	Old Gold–vy. lt.
891		676	Old Gold–lt.
887		3046	Yellow Beige–med.
373		3045	Yellow Beige–dk.
366		951	Peach Pecan–lt.
881		945	Peach Beige
11		3328	Salmon–dk.
49		3689	Mauve–lt.
969		316	Antique Mauve–med.
117		3747	Blue Violet–vy. lt.

118		340	Blue Violet–med.
940		3807	Cornflower Blue
843		3364	Pine Green
311		3827	Golden Brown–pale
363		436	Tan
375		420	Hazel Nut Brown–dk.
899		3782	Mocha Brown–lt.

Step 2:　Backstitch (1 strand)

891		676	Old Gold–lt.
101		327	Antique Violet–vy. dk.
940		3807	Cornflower Blue
843		3364	Pine Green
324		922	Copper–lt. (2 strands)
382		3021	Brown Gray–vy. dk.

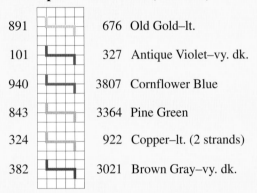

Stitch Count: 60 width x 70 length

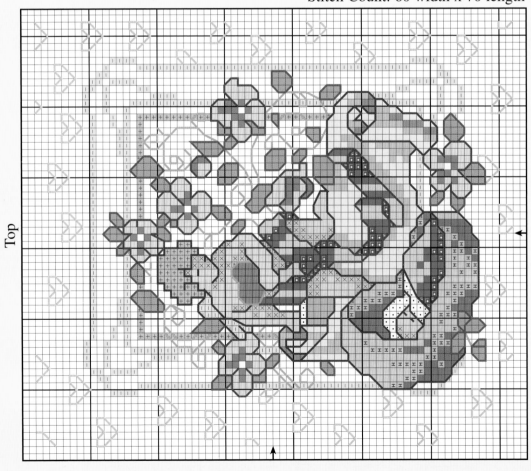

Top

The sample was stitched on White Cashel Linen
28 over 2. The finished design size is 4¼" x 5".
The fabric was cut 11" x 11".

Anchor   **DMC**

Step 1: Cross-stitch (2 strands)

Anchor			DMC	
1				White
300			745	Yellow–lt. pale
306			3820	Straw–dk.
366			951	Peach Pecan–lt.
11			351	Coral
13			349	Coral–dk.
22			816	Garnet
72			902	Garnet–vy. dk.
158			775	Baby Blue–vy. lt.
167			519	Sky Blue
130			799	Delft–med.
843			3364	Pine Green

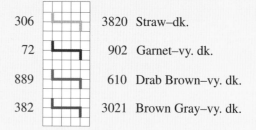

Anchor			DMC	
861			3363	Pine Green–med.
215			320	Pistachio Green–med.
878			501	Blue Green–dk.
830			644	Beige Gray–med.
392			642	Beige Gray–dk.
403			310	Black

Step 2: Backstitch (1 strand)

Anchor		DMC	
306		3820	Straw–dk.
72		902	Garnet–vy. dk.
889		610	Drab Brown–vy. dk.
382		3021	Brown Gray–vy. dk.

Step 3: French Knot (1 strand)

Anchor		DMC	
13		349	Coral–dk.
889		610	Drab Brown–vy. dk.

Stitch Count: 60 width x 70 length

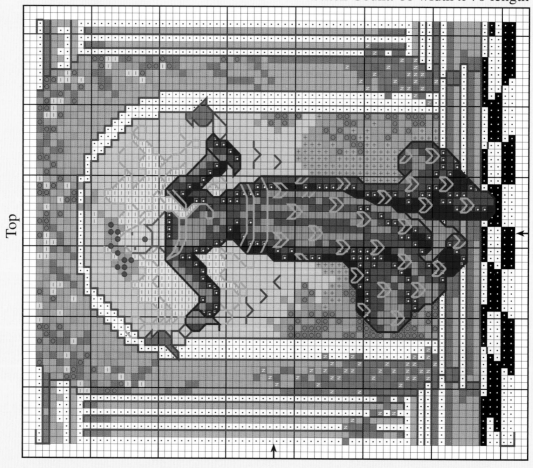

Top

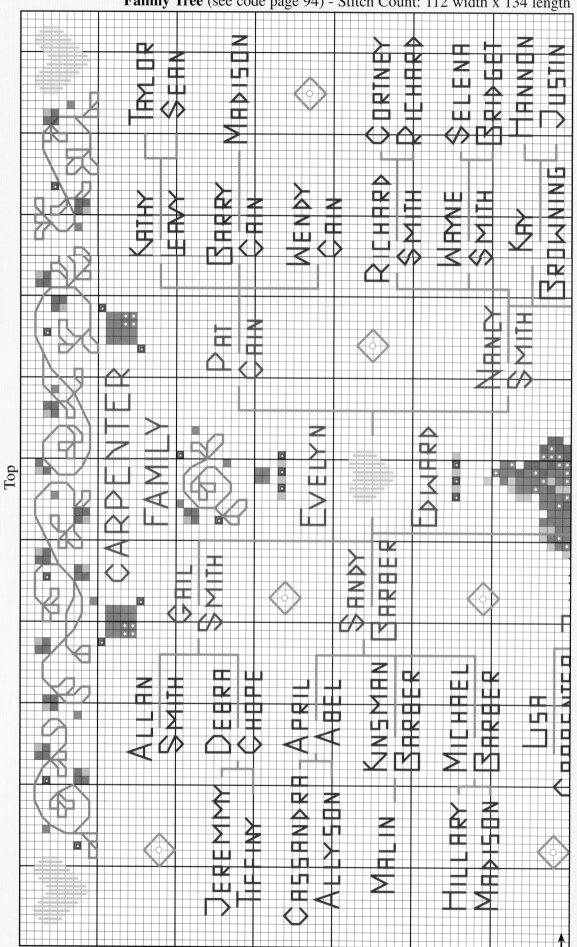

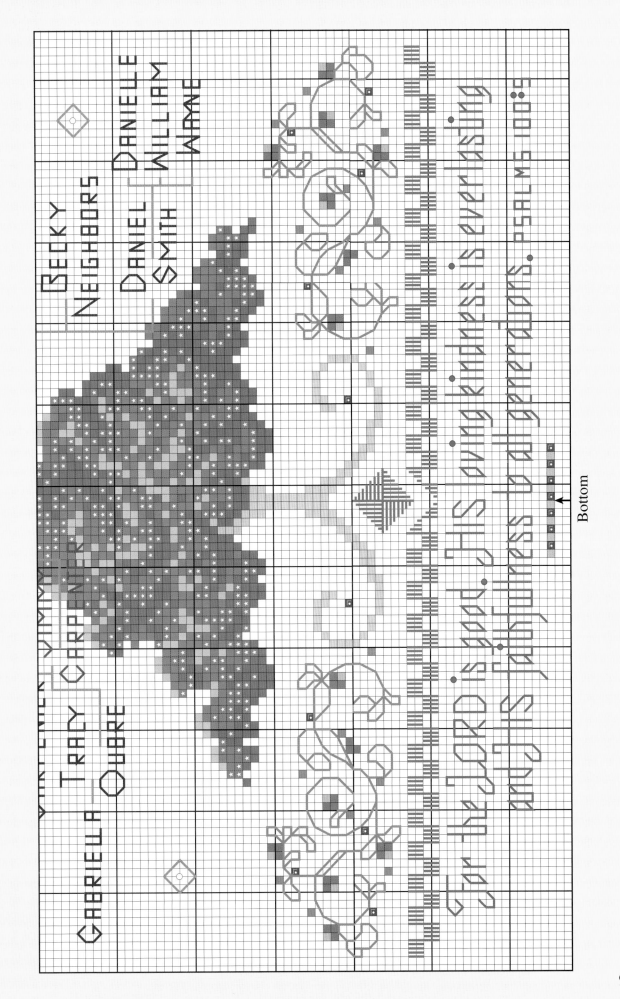

Bottom

Family Tree

The sample was stitched on Antique Rose Linen 28 over 2. The finished design size is 8" x 9⅝". The fabric was cut 14" x 16".

Anchor		DMC	

Step 1: Cross-stitch (2 strands)

Anchor		DMC	
891		676	Old Gold–lt.
894		223	Shell Pink–med.
872		3740	Antique Violet–dk.
161		826	Blue–med.
921		931	Antique Blue–med.
900		928	Slate Green–lt.
900		928	Slate Green–lt. (1 strand)
779		926	Slate Green (1 strand)
779		926	Slate Green
388		3033	Mocha Brown–vy. lt.
942		738	Tan–vy. lt.

Step 2: Backstitch (1 strand)

Anchor		DMC	
70		3685	Mauve–dk.
872		3740	Antique Violet–dk. (2 strands) (CARPENTER FAMILY)
872		3740	Antique Violet–dk.
779		926	Slate Green (2 strands)
840		3768	Slate Green–dk.
832		612	Drab Brown–med. (2 strands)

Step 3: French Knot (1 strand)

Anchor		DMC	
840		3768	Slate Green–dk.

Step 4: Long Stitch (1 strand)

Anchor		DMC	
832		612	Drab Brown–med.

Step 5: Satin Stitch (2 strands)

Anchor		DMC	
		91	Blue Varigated
388		3033	Mocha Brown–vy. lt.

Step 6: Beadwork

		02010	Ice

Little Red Church

See photo, page 1. The sample was stitched on Yellow Pastel Linen 28 over 2. The finished design size is 5⅝" x 5⅞". The fabric was cut 16" x 16".

Anchor		DMC	

Step 1: Cross-stitch (2 strands)

Anchor		DMC	
1			White
893		224	Shell Pink–lt. (1 strand)
894		223	Shell Pink–med. (1 strand)
896		3722	Shell Pink
1019		3802	Antique Mauve–deep
872		3740	Antique Violet–dk.
130		799	Delft–med.
264		472	Avocado Green–ultra lt.
860		3053	Green Gray
214		368	Pistachio Green–lt.
215		320	Pistachio Green–med. (1 strand)
840		3768	Slate Green–dk. (1 strand)
876		502	Blue Green
876		502	Blue Green (1 strand)
266		3347	Yellow Green–med. (1 strand)
878		501	Blue Green–dk.
840		3768	Slate Green–dk.
851		924	Slate Green–vy. dk.
363		436	Tan
370		434	Brown–lt. (1 strand)
393		3790	Beige Gray–ultra vy. dk. (1 strand)
375		420	Hazel Nut Brown–dk.
388		3033	Mocha Brown–vy. lt. (1 strand)
899		3782	Mocha Brown–lt. (1 strand)
905		3781	Mocha Brown–dk.
900		3024	Brown Gray–vy. lt.
8581		647	Beaver Gray–med.

Step 2: Backstitch (1 strand)

Anchor		DMC	
1			White
905		3781	Mocha Brown–dk.
382		3371	Black Brown

Step 3: French Knot (1 strand)

Anchor		DMC	
905		3781	Mocha Brown–dk.
382		3371	Black Brown

Little Red Church - Stitch Count: 78 width x 82 length

Step 4: Long Stitch (2 strands)

1   White

A Christmas Sampler

The sample was stitched on Mushroom/Gold Lugana 25 over 2. The finished design size is 11½" x 15⅝". The fabric was cut 18" x 22".

Anchor | **DMC**

Step 1: Cross Stitch (2 strands)

Anchor		DMC	
1			White
926			Ecru
300		745	Yellow–lt. pale
305		3822	Straw–lt.
886		677	Old Gold–vy. lt.
886		677	Old Gold–vy. lt. (1 strand)
306		725	Topaz (1 strand)
891		676	Old Gold–lt.
891		676	Old Gold–lt. (1 strand)
890		729	Old Gold–med. (1 strand)
890		729	Old Gold–med.
890		729	Old Gold–med. (1 strand)
308		782	Topaz–med. (1 strand)
890		729	Old Gold–med. (1 strand)
375		420	Hazel Nut Brown–dk. (1 strand)
307		783	Christmas Gold
307		783	Christmas Gold (1 strand)
306		725	Topaz (1 strand)
308		782	Topaz–med.
309		781	Topaz–dk.
10		352	Coral–lt.
11		351	Coral
10		3712	Salmon–med.
13		347	Salmon–vy. dk.
892		225	Shell Pink–vy. lt.
893		224	Shell Pink–lt.
894		223	Shell Pink–med. (1 strand)
25		3326	Rose–lt. (1 strand)
896		3722	Shell Pink (1 strand)
27		899	Rose–med. (1 strand)
896		3721	Shell Pink–dk.
49		963	Wild Rose–vy. lt.
49		963	Wild Rose–vy. lt. (1 strand)
8		761	Salmon–lt. (1 strand)
25		3326	Rose–lt. (1 strand)
27		899	Rose–med. (1 strand)
27		899	Rose–med. (1 strand)
896		3722	Shell Pink (1 strand)
74		3354	Dusty Rose–vy. lt. (1 strand)
9		760	Salmon (1 strand)
75		3733	Dusty Rose–lt.
1014		3830	Terra Cotta
22		816	Garnet
44		814	Garnet–dk.
969		316	Antique Mauve–med.
117		3747	Blue Violet–vy. lt.
108		211	Lavender–lt.
108		211	Lavender–lt. (1 strand)
117		341	Blue Violet–lt. (1 strand)
117		341	Blue Violet–lt.
117		341	Blue Violet–lt. (1 strand)
121		793	Cornflower Blue–med. (1 strand)
158		3756	Baby Blue–ultra vy. lt.
158		775	Baby Blue–vy. lt.
159		3325	Baby Blue–lt.
343		3752	Antique Blue–vy. lt.
920		932	Antique Blue–lt.
921		931	Antique Blue–med.
922		930	Antique Blue–dk.
816		3750	Antique Blue–vy. dk.
121		793	Cornflower Blue–med.
940		792	Cornflower Blue–dk.
214		368	Pistachio Green–lt. (1 strand)
265		3348	Yellow Green–lt. (1 strand)
215		320	Pistachio Green–med.
265		3348	Yellow Green–lt.
265		3348	Yellow Green–lt. (1 strand)
843		3364	Pine Green (1 strand)
266		3347	Yellow Green–med.
843		3364	Pine Green
861		3363	Pine Green–med.
861		3363	Pine Green–med. (1 strand)
846		3051	Green Gray–dk. (1 strand)
842		3013	Khaki Green–lt.
842		3013	Khaki Green–lt. (1 strand)
264		472	Avocado Green–ultra lt. (1 strand)
859		3052	Green Gray–dk.
846		3051	Green Gray–dk.
876		502	Blue Green
878		501	Blue Green–dk.
840		3768	Slate Green–dk.
851		924	Slate Green–vy. dk. (1 strand)
846		3051	Green Gray–dk. (1 strand)

97

373	A	422 Hazel Nut Brown–lt.
375		420 Hazel Nut Brown–dk.
363		436 Tan
309		435 Brown–vy. lt.
309	♥	435 Brown–vy. lt. (1 strand)
351		400 Mahogany–dk. (1 strand)
351		400 Mahogany–dk.
900		3024 Brown Gray–vy. lt.
388	✳	3033 Mocha Brown–vy. lt.
392	H	642 Beige Gray–dk.
903		640 Beige Gray–vy. dk.
899		3782 Mocha Brown–lt.
376	W	842 Beige Brown–vy. lt.
889		610 Drab Brown–vy. dk.
905		3031 Mocha Brown–vy. dk.
236		3799 Pewter Gray–vy. dk.
403		310 Black

Step 2: Backstitch (1 strand)

926	Ecru
307	783 Christmas Gold (2 strands)
308	782 Topaz–med.
309	781 Topaz–dk. (2 strands)
970	3726 Antique Mauve–dk.
1019	3802 Antique Mauve–deep (2 strands)
78	3803 Mauve–dk.
44	814 Garnet–dk. (2 strands)
72	902 Garnet–vy. dk.
872	3740 Antique Violet–dk.
	103 Blue–dk. Varigated

922	930 Antique Blue–dk.
816	3750 Antique Blue–vy. dk.
940	792 Cornflower Blue–dk.
846	3051 Green Gray–dk.
862	935 Avocado Green–dk.
878	501 Blue Green–dk.
840	3768 Slate Green–dk.
851	924 Slate Green–vy. dk.
387	822 Beige Gray–lt. (2 strands)
392	642 Beige Gray–dk.
889	610 Drab Brown–vy. dk.
904	3781 Mocha Brown–dk.
905	3031 Mocha Brown–vy. dk.
236	3799 Pewter Gray–vy. dk.

Step 3: French Knot (1 strand)

926	Ecru
11	350 Coral–med.
969	3727 Antique Mauve–lt.
78	3803 Mauve–dk.
843	3364 Pine Green
	103 Blue–dk. Varigated
889	610 Drab Brown–vy. dk.
904	3781 Mocha Brown–dk.
236	3799 Pewter Gray–vy. dk.

Step 4: Beadwork

	02010 Ice

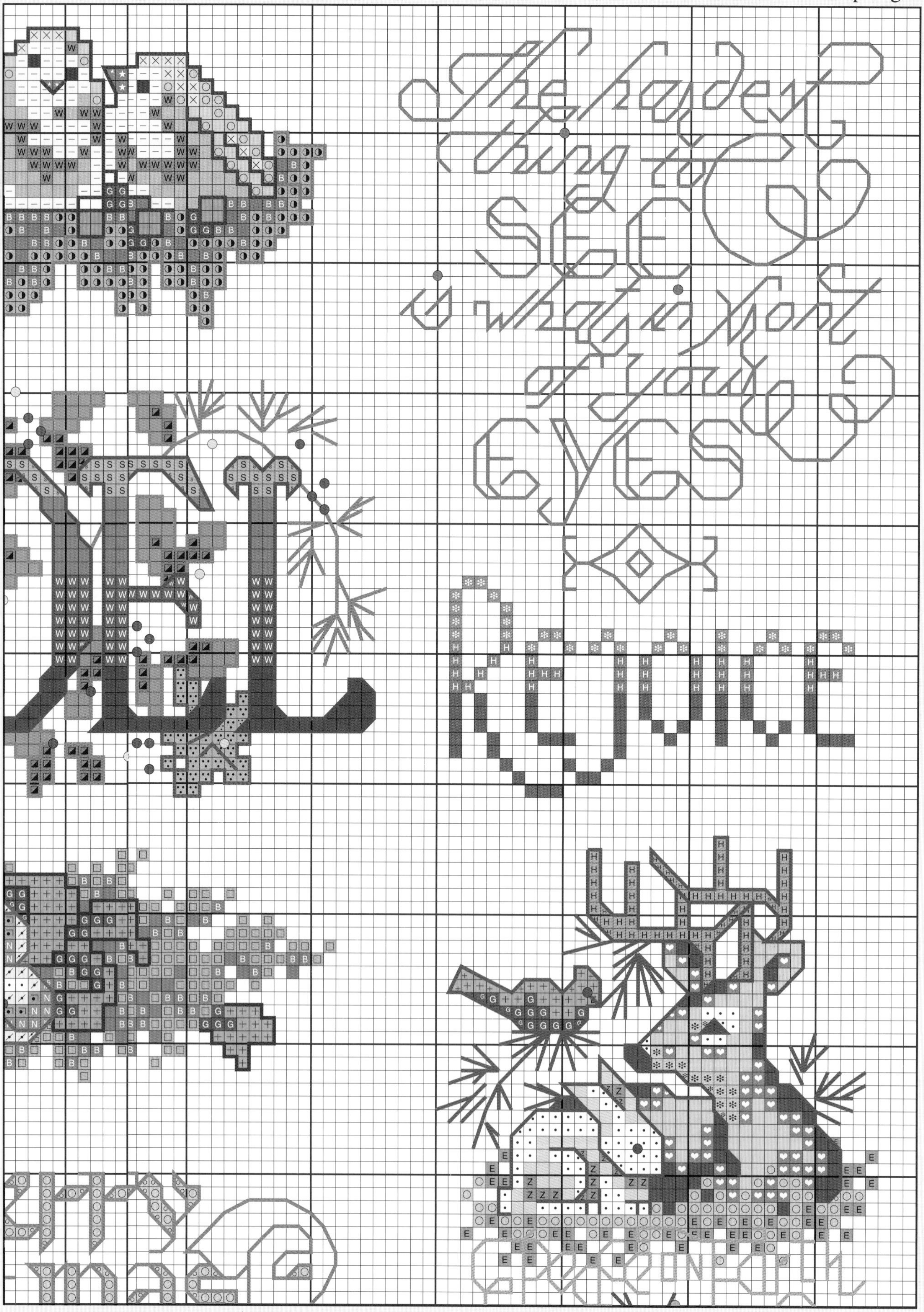

Make &
new Friends
But Keep the Old
One is Silver
& the
Gold.
other
is

Bottom Left

101

A Floral Sampler

The sampler was not stitched in its entirety. The mini-design of the Floral Tea Towel was stitched on White Aida Tea Towel 14 over 1. The finished design size is 3¼" x 1⅜".

Anchor   **DMC**

Step 1: Cross-stitch (2 strands)

Anchor	DMC	Color
1		White
926		Ecru
300	3823	Yellow–ultra pale
300	745	Yellow–lt. pale
305	3822	Straw–lt.
907	3821	Straw
306	3820	Straw–dk.
886	677	Old Gold–vy. lt.
891	676	Old Gold–lt.
891	676	Old Gold–lt. (1 strand)
300	745	Yellow–lt. pale (1 strand)
890	729	Old Gold–med.
307	783	Christmas Gold
886	3047	Yellow Beige–lt.
881	945	Peach Beige
8	761	Salmon–lt.
11	3328	Salmon–dk.
10	352	Coral–lt.
11	351	Coral
11	350	Coral–med. (1 strand)
896	3721	Shell Pink–dk. (1 strand)
892	225	Shell Pink–vy. lt.
892	225	Shell Pink–vy. lt. (1 strand)
8	761	Salmon–lt. (1 strand)
893	224	Shell Pink–lt.
893	224	Shell Pink–lt. (1 strand)
894	223	Shell Pink–med. (1 strand)
894	223	Shell Pink–med.
896	3722	Shell Pink
49	963	Wild Rose–vy. lt.
49	963	Wild Rose–vy. lt. (1 strand)
108	211	Lavender–lt. (1 strand)
25	3326	Rose–lt.
25	3326	Rose–lt. (1 strand)
27	899	Rose–med. (1 strand)
969	3727	Antique Mauve–lt.
969	316	Antique Mauve–med.
969	316	Antique Mauve–med. (1 strand)
8	761	Salmon–lt. (1 strand)
970	3726	Antique Mauve–dk. (1 strand)
69	3687	Mauve (1 strand)
108	211	Lavender–lt.
104	210	Lavender–med.
104	210	Lavender–med. (1 strand)
108	211	Lavender–lt. (1 strand)
870	3042	Antique Violet–lt.
870	3042	Antique Violet–lt. (1 strand)
118	340	Blue Violet–med. (1 strand)
871	3041	Antique Violet–med.
872	3740	Antique Violet–dk. (1 strand)
110	208	Lavender–vy. dk. (1 strand)
117	3747	Blue Violet–vy. lt.
117	3747	Blue Violet–vy. lt. (1 strand)
158	775	Baby Blue–vy. lt. (1 strand)
117	341	Blue Violet–lt.
117	341	Blue Violet–lt. (1 strand)
104	210	Lavender–med. (1 strand)
117	341	Blue Violet–lt. (1 strand)
118	340	Blue Violet–med. (1 strand)
118	340	Blue Violet–med.
160	3761	Sky Blue–lt.
167	519	Sky Blue
158	775	Baby Blue–vy. lt.
159	3325	Baby Blue–lt.
975	3753	Antique Blue–ultra vy. lt.
121	793	Cornflower Blue–med.
940	792	Cornflower Blue–dk.
940	792	Cornflower Blue–dk. (1 strand)
118	340	Blue Violet–med. (1 strand)
876	502	Blue Green
878	501	Blue Green–dk.
878	501	Blue Green–dk. (1 strand)
861	3363	Pine Green–med. (1 strand)
779	926	Slate Green
840	3768	Slate Green–dk.
859	522	Fern Green
843	3364	Pine Green
843	3364	Pine Green (1 strand)
264	472	Avocado Green–ultra lt. (1 strand)
861	3363	Pine Green–med.
861	3363	Pine Green–med. (1 strand)
266	3347	Yellow Green–med. (1 strand)

264	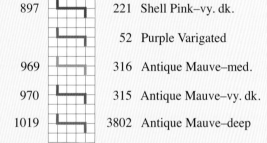	472	Avocado Green–ultra lt.
859		3052	Green Gray–med.
265		3348	Yellow Green–lt.
842		3013	Khaki Green–lt. (1 strand)
267		470	Avocado Green–lt. (1 strand)
844		3012	Khaki Green–med.
215		3aa20	Pistachio Green–med.
246		319	Pistachio Green–vy. dk.
311		3827	Golden Brown–pale
307		977	Golden Brown–lt.
832		612	Drab Brown–med.
373		422	Hazel Nut Brown–lt.
375		420	Hazel Nut Brown–dk.
375		420	Hazel Nut Brown–dk. (1 strand)
373		422	Hazel Nut Brown–lt. (1 strand)
944		869	Hazel Nut Brown–vy. dk.
899		3782	Mocha Brown–lt.
403		310	Black

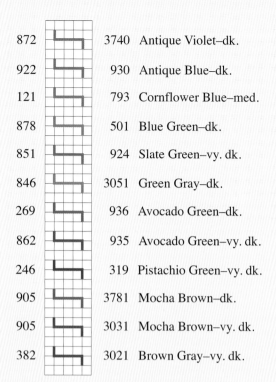

872	3740	Antique Violet–dk.
922	930	Antique Blue–dk.
121	793	Cornflower Blue–med.
878	501	Blue Green–dk.
851	924	Slate Green–vy. dk.
846	3051	Green Gray–dk.
269	936	Avocado Green–dk.
862	935	Avocado Green–vy. dk.
246	319	Pistachio Green–vy. dk.
905	3781	Mocha Brown–dk.
905	3031	Mocha Brown–vy. dk.
382	3021	Brown Gray–vy. dk.

Step 2: Backstitch (1 strand)

897	221	Shell Pink–vy. dk.
	52	Purple Varigated
969	316	Antique Mauve–med.
970	315	Antique Mauve–vy. dk.
1019	3802	Antique Mauve–deep

Step 3: French Knot (1 strand)

892	225	Shell Pink–vy. lt.
922	930	Antique Blue–dk.
905	3781	Mocha Brown–dk.

Step 4: Beadwork

| 00151 | Ash Mauve |
| 00358 | Cobalt Blue |

Those who
plant kindness
harvest Love

To every thing
there is a season
and a time to every purpose
under the heaven.
Eccl. 3:1

Bottom Left

Bottom Right

A Winter Sampler

The sampler was not stitched in its entirety. The mini-design of Santa with the animals was stitched on White Cashel Linen 28 over 2. The finished design size is 2¾" x 3⅜". The fabric was cut 9" x 10".

Anchor   **DMC**

Step 1:   Cross-stitch (2 strands)

Anchor		DMC	
1			White
926			Ecru
300		745	Yellow–lt. pale
305		3822	Straw–lt.
907		3821	Straw
306		3820	Straw–dk.
886		677	Old Gold–vy. lt.
886		677	Old Gold–vy. lt. (1 strand)
386		746	Off White (1 strand)
891		676	Old Gold–lt.
890		729	Old Gold–med.
373		3045	Yellow Beige–dk.
307		783	Christmas Gold
307		783	Christmas Gold (1 strand)
306		725	Topaz (1 strand)
881		945	Peach Beige
4146		754	Peach–lt.
324		721	Orange Spice–med.
9		760	Salmon
10		3712	Salmon–med.
11		3328	Salmon–dk.
13		347	Salmon–vy. dk.
10		351	Coral
11		350	Coral–med.
20		498	Christmas Red–dk.
22		816	Garnet
49		963	Wild Rose–vy. lt.
25		3326	Rose–lt.
27		899	Rose–med.
42		335	Rose
76		3731	Dusty Rose–med.
892		225	Shell Pink–vy. lt.
894		223	Shell Pink–med.
75		604	Cranberry–lt.
69		3687	Mauve
78		3803	Mauve–dk.

Anchor		DMC	
969		316	Antique Mauve–med.
970		315	Antique Mauve–vy. dk.
86		3608	Plum–vy. lt.
87		3607	Plum–lt.
88		718	Plum
108		211	Lavender–lt.
104		210	Lavender–med.
871		3041	Antique Violet–med.
872		3740	Antique Violet–dk.
117		3747	Blue Violet–vy. lt.
117		3747	Blue Violet–vy. lt. (1 strand)
1			White (1 strand)
117		341	Blue Violet–lt.
118		340	Blue Violet–med.
118		340	Blue Violet–med. (1 strand)
117		3747	Blue Violet–vy. lt. (1 strand)
119		333	Blue Violet–vy. dk.
158		775	Baby Blue–vy. lt.
159		3325	Baby Blue–lt.
121		794	Cornflower Blue–lt.
121		793	Cornflower Blue–med.
940		3807	Cornflower Blue
130		799	Delft–med.
131		798	Delft–dk.
132		797	Royal Blue
975		3753	Antique Blue–ultra vy. lt.
922		930	Antique Blue–dk.
167		519	Sky Blue
167		3766	Peacock Blue–lt.
214		368	Pistachio Green–lt.
208		563	Jade–lt.
279		734	Olive Green–lt.
266		581	Moss Green
858		524	Fern Green–vy. lt.
843		3364	Pine Green
843		3364	Pine Green (1 strand)
266		471	Avocado Green–vy. lt. (1 strand)
861		3363	Pine Green–med.
859		3052	Green Gray–med.
266		3347	Yellow Green–med.
876		502	Blue Green
878		501	Blue Green–dk.
877		3815	Celadon Green–dk.
387		822	Beige Gray–lt.
324		922	Copper–lt.

338		3776	Mahogany–lt.
942		738	Tan–vy. lt.
362		437	Tan–lt.
363		436	Tan
309		435	Brown–vy. lt.
388		3033	Mocha Brown–vy. lt.
899		3782	Mocha Brown–lt.
373		422	Hazel Nut Brown–lt.
956		613	Drab Brown–lt.
832		612	Drab Brown–med.
898		611	Drab Brown–dk.
888		3828	Hazel Nut Brown
936		632	Pecan–dk.
376		842	Beige Brown–vy. lt.
1014		3830	Terra Cotta
382		3371	Black Brown
830		644	Beige Gray–med.
397		3072	Beaver Gray–vy. lt.
900		648	Beaver Gray–lt.
8581		647	Beaver Gray–med.
900		3024	Brown Gray–vy. lt.
8581		3022	Brown Gray–med.
397		762	Pearl Gray–vy. lt.
398		415	Pearl Gray
403		310	Black

Step 2: Backstitch (1 strand)

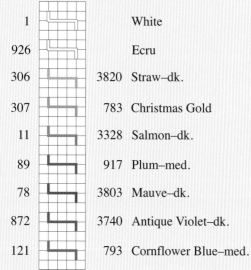

1			White
926			Ecru
306		3820	Straw–dk.
307		783	Christmas Gold
11		3328	Salmon–dk.
89		917	Plum–med.
78		3803	Mauve–dk.
872		3740	Antique Violet–dk.
121		793	Cornflower Blue–med.

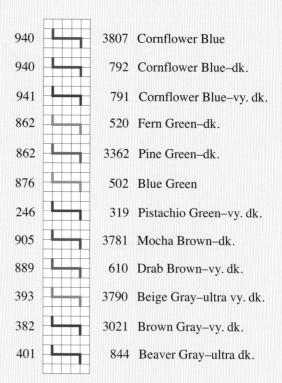

940		3807	Cornflower Blue
940		792	Cornflower Blue–dk.
941		791	Cornflower Blue–vy. dk.
862		520	Fern Green–dk.
862		3362	Pine Green–dk.
876		502	Blue Green
246		319	Pistachio Green–vy. dk.
905		3781	Mocha Brown–dk.
889		610	Drab Brown–vy. dk.
393		3790	Beige Gray–ultra vy. dk.
382		3021	Brown Gray–vy. dk.
401		844	Beaver Gray–ultra dk.

Step 3: French Knot (1 strand)

1			White
926			Ecru
324		721	Orange Spice–med.
13		349	Coral–dk.
118		340	Blue Violet–med.
382		3371	Black Brown
905		3781	Mocha Brown–dk.
393		3790	Beige Gray–ultra vy. dk.
382		3021	Brown Gray–vy. dk.

Step 4: Long Stitch (1 strand)

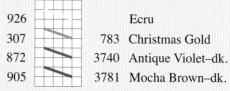

926			Ecru
307		783	Christmas Gold
872		3740	Antique Violet–dk.
905		3781	Mocha Brown–dk.

Step 5: Beadwork

	02010	Ice
	02011	Victorian Gold

Stitch Count: 138 width x 186 length

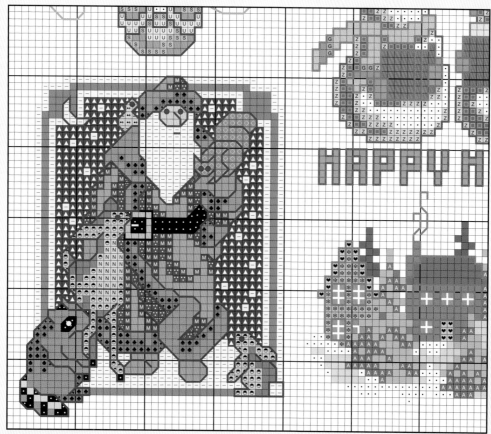

Bottom Left

Bottom Right

A Bear Sampler

The sampler was not stitched in its entirety. The mini-design of the angel with verse was stitched on Cream Silk Canvas 24 over 2. The finished design size is 3¾" x 4¼". The fabric was cut 10" x 11". The floral heart was stitched on Cream Cashel Linen 28 over 2. The finished design size is 2⅞" x 2½". The fabric was cut fabric 9" x 9".

Anchor		DMC	

Step 1: Cross-stitch (2 strands)

Anchor		DMC	
1			White
926			Ecru
387		712	Cream
387		712	Cream (1 strand)
117		3747	Blue Violet–vy. lt. (1 strand)
386		746	Off White (1 strand)
300		745	Yellow–lt. pale (1 strand)
300		745	Yellow–lt. pale
306		725	Topaz
907		3821	Straw
886		677	Old Gold–vy. lt.
886		677	Old Gold–vy. lt. (1 strand)
891		676	Old Gold–lt. (1 strand)
891		676	Old Gold–lt.
890		729	Old Gold–med.
307		783	Christmas Gold
881		945	Peach Beige
49		963	Wild Rose–vy. lt.
25		3326	Rose–lt.
25		3326	Rose–lt. (1 strand)
9		760	Salmon (1 strand)
27		899	Rose–med. (1 strand)
76		3731	Dusty Rose–med. (1 strand)
8		761	Salmon–lt.
9		760	Salmon
10		3712	Salmon–med.
10		3712	Salmon–med. (1 strand)
894		223	Shell Pink–med. (1 strand)
11		3328	Salmon–dk.
11		351	Coral
894		223	Shell Pink–med.
896		3722	Shell Pink
897		221	Shell Pink–vy. dk.

Anchor		DMC	
85		3609	Plum–ultra lt. (1 strand)
66		3688	Mauve–med. (1 strand)
87		3607	Plum–lt. (1 strand)
69		3687	Mauve (1 strand)
49		3689	Mauve–lt. (1 strand)
969		3727	Antique Mauve–lt. (1 strand)
66		3688	Mauve–med.
69		3687	Mauve
78		3803	Mauve–dk.
78		3803	Mauve–dk. (1 strand)
101		327	Antique Violet–vy. dk. (1 strand)
969		316	Antique Mauve–med.
108		211	Lavender–lt.
117		3747	Blue Violet–vy. lt.
872		3740	Antique Violet–dk.
101		327	Antique Violet–vy. dk.
158		3756	Baby Blue–ultra vy. lt.
158		3756	Baby Blue–ultra vy. lt. (1 strand)
128		800	Delft–pale (1 strand)
158		775	Baby Blue–vy. lt.
158		775	Baby Blue–vy. lt. (1 strand)
159		3325	Baby Blue–lt. (1 strand)
158		775	Baby Blue–vy. lt. (1 strand)
128		800	Delft–pale (1 strand)
159		3325	Baby Blue–lt.
154		3755	Baby Blue
154		3755	Baby Blue (1 strand)
145		334	Baby Blue–med. (1 strand)
145		334	Baby Blue–med.
128		800	Delft–pale
121		794	Cornflower Blue–lt.
978		322	Navy Blue–vy. lt. (1 strand)
921		931	Antique Blue–med. (1 strand)
978		322	Navy Blue–vy. lt. (1 strand)
147		312	Navy Blue–lt. (1 strand)
921		931	Antique Blue–med.
132		797	Royal Blue
149		311	Navy Blue–med.
185		964	Seagreen–lt.
849		927	Slate Green–med.
779		926	Slate Green
840		3768	Slate Green–dk.
840		3768	Slate Green–dk. (1 strand)
879		500	Blue Green–vy. dk. (1 strand)

858		524	Fern Green–vy. lt.
859		523	Fern Green–lt.
859		522	Fern Green
842		3013	Khaki Green–lt.
844		3012	Khaki Green–med.
265		3348	Yellow Green–lt.
265 / 843		3348 / 3364	Yellow Green–lt. (1 strand) / Pine Green (1 strand)
215		320	Pistachio Green–med.
264		472	Avocado Green–ultra lt.
859		3052	Green Gray–med.
843		3364	Pine Green
861		3363	Pine Green–med.
861 / 876		3363 / 502	Pine Green–med. (1 strand) / Blue Green (1 strand)
217		3817	Celadon Green–lt.
213		504	Blue Green–lt.
876		502	Blue Green
311		3827	Golden Brown–pale
307		977	Golden Brown–lt.
347		402	Mahogany–vy. lt.
338		3776	Mahogany–lt.
338 / 309		3776 / 435	Mahogany–lt. (1 strand) / Brown–vy. lt. (1 strand)
362		437	Tan–lt.
363		436	Tan
363 / 309		436 / 435	Tan (1 strand) / Brown–vy. lt. (1 strand)
370		434	Brown–lt.
373		422	Hazel Nut Brown–lt.
373 / 890		422 / 729	Hazel Nut Brown–lt. (1 strand) / Old Gold–med. (1 strand)
888		3828	Hazel Nut Brown
375		420	Hazel Nut Brown–dk.
375 / 890		420 / 729	Hazel Nut Brown–dk. (1 strand) / Old Gold–med. (1 strand)
832 / 898		612 / 611	Drab Brown–med. (1 strand) / Drab Brown–dk. (1 strand)
388 / 900		3033 / 3024	Mocha Brown–vy. lt. (1 strand) / Brown Gray–vy. lt. (1 strand)
905 / 273		3031 / 3787	Mocha Brown–vy. dk. (1 strand) / Brown Gray–dk. (1 strand)
376		842	Beige Brown–vy. lt.
378		841	Beige Brown–lt.
379		840	Beige Brown–med.
382		3371	Black Brown
387		822	Beige Gray–lt.
900		648	Beaver Gray–lt.

900 / 8581		648 / 647	Beaver Gray–lt. (1 strand) / Beaver Gray–med. (1 strand)
900 / 397		648 / 3072	Beaver Gray–lt. (1 strand) / Beaver Gray–vy. lt. (1 strand)
8581		647	Beaver Gray–med.
900		3024	Brown Gray–vy. lt.
8581		3023	Brown Gray–lt.

Step 2:   Backstitch (1 strand)

387		712	Cream
907		3821	Straw
309		781	Topaz–dk.
9		760	Salmon
894		223	Shell Pink–med.
78		3803	Mauve–dk.
70		3685	Mauve–vy. dk.
970		315	Antique Mauve–vy. dk.
872		3740	Antique Violet–dk.
101		327	Antique Violet–vy. dk.
150		823	Navy Blue–dk.
851		924	Slate Green–vy. dk.
269		936	Avocado Green–vy. dk.
862		3362	Pine Green–dk.
879		500	Blue Green–vy. dk.
375		420	Hazel Nut Brown–dk.
905		3031	Mocha Brown–vy. dk.
380		839	Beige Brown–dk.
382		3371	Black Brown
273		3787	Brown Gray–dk.
382		3021	Brown Gray–vy. dk.

Step 3:   French Knot (1 strand)

78		3803	Mauve–dk.
872		3740	Antique Violet–dk.
970		315	Antique Mauve–vy. dk.
150		823	Navy Blue–dk.
905		3031	Mocha Brown–vy. dk.
380		839	Beige Brown dk.

This
is the day
which the Lord
hath made:
we will rejoice
and be glad in it.

Psalm 118:24

Believe

| 382 | | 3021 | Brown Gray–vy. dk. |

Step 4: Long Stitch (1 strand)

| 1 | | | White |
| 309 | | 781 | Topaz–dk. |

Bless our Family

Blessed

An Alphabet Sampler

The sampler was not stitched in its entirety. The mini-design of the Peace of Earth Angel was stitched on Pearly Grey Cashel Linen 28 over 2. The finished design size is 2¾" x 4". The fabric was cut 9" x 10".

Anchor   DMC

Step 1:   Cross-stitch (2 strands)

Anchor	DMC	
1		White
387	712	Cream
300	745	Yellow–lt. pale
886	677	Old Gold–vy. lt.
891	676	Old Gold–lt.
907	3821	Straw
307	783	Christmas Gold
307	783	Christmas Gold (1 strand)
306	725	Topaz (1 strand)
308	782	Topaz–med.
366	951	Peach Beige–lt.
881	945	Peach Beige
881	945	Peach Beige (1 strand)
882	3773	Pecan–vy. lt. (1 strand)
48	818	Baby Pink
49	963	Wild Rose–vy. lt.
49	963	Wild Rose–vy. lt. (1 strand)
85	3609	Plum–ultra lt. (1 strand)
24	776	Pink–med.
25	3326	Rose–lt.
25	3326	Rose–lt. (1 strand)
27	899	Rose–med. (1 strand)
25	3326	Rose–lt. (1 strand)
894	223	Shell Pink–med. (1 strand)
27	899	Rose–med.
76	3731	Dusty Rose–med.
10	3712	Salmon–med.
11	3328	Salmon–dk.
11	351	Coral
49	3689	Mauve–lt. (1 strand)
66	3688	Mauve–med. (1 strand)
66	3688	Mauve–med.
66	3688	Mauve–med. (1 strand)
105	209	Lavender–dk. (1 strand)
69	3687	Mauve

Anchor	DMC	
69	3687	Mauve (1 strand)
86	3608	Plum–vy. lt. (1 strand)
69	3687	Mauve (1 strand)
970	3726	Antique Mauve–dk. (1 strand)
70	3685	Mauve–vy. dk. (1 strand)
86	3608	Plum–vy. lt.
894	223	Shell Pink–med.
896	3722	Shell Pink
1014	3830	Terra Cotta (1 strand)
970	3726	Antique Mauve–dk.
78	3803	Mauve–dk.
108	211	Lavender–lt.
105	209	Lavender–dk.
95	554	Violet–lt.
95	554	Violet–lt. (1 strand)
118	340	Blue Violet–med. (1 strand)
99	552	Violet–dk.
871	3041	Antique Violet–med.
871	3041	Antique Violet–med. (1 strand)
119	333	Blue Violet–vy. dk. (1 strand)
872	3740	Antique Violet–dk.
117	3747	Blue Violet–vy. lt.
119	3746	Blue Violet–dk.
119	333	Blue Violet–vy. dk.
158	3756	Baby Blue–ultra vy. lt.
158	775	Baby Blue–vy. lt.
128	800	Delft–pale
154	3755	Baby Blue
978	322	Navy Blue–vy. lt.
121	793	Cornflower Blue–med.
940	3807	Cornflower Blue
185	964	Seagreen–lt.
779	926	Slate Green
265	3348	Yellow Green–lt.
842	3013	Khaki Green–lt.
842	3013	Khaki Green–lt. (1 strand)
844	3012	Khaki Green–med. (1 strand)
844	3012	Khaki Green–med.
843	3364	Pine Green
843	3364	Pine Green (1 strand)
861	3363	Pine Green–med. (1 strand)
861	3363	Pine Green–med.
862	3362	Pine Green–dk.

862		3362	Pine Green–dk. (1 strand)
879		500	Blue Green–vy. dk. (1 strand)
215		320	Pistachio Green–med.
387		822	Beige Gray–lt.
942		738	Tan–vy. lt.
311		3827	Golden Brown–pale
373		422	Hazel Nut Brown–lt.
888		3828	Hazel Nut Brown
309		435	Brown–vy. lt.
371		433	Brown–med.
1014		3830	Terra Cotta
376		842	Beige Brown–vy. lt.
378		841	Beige Brown–lt.
899		3782	Mocha Brown–lt.
905		3781	Mocha Brown–dk.
397		3072	Beaver Gray–vy. lt.
900		648	Beaver Gray–lt.

Step 2: Backstitch (1 strand)

387		712	Cream
307		783	Christmas Gold
308		782	Topaz–med.
1019		3802	Antique Mauve–deep
101		327	Antique Violet–vy. dk.
894		223	Shell Pink–med.
896		3722	Shell Pink
78		3803	Mauve–dk.
101		550	Violet–vy. dk.
119		333	Blue Violet–vy. dk.
872		3740	Antique Violet–dk.
922		930	Antique Blue–dk.

149		336	Navy Blue
851		924	Slate Green–vy. dk.
1068		3808	Turquoise–ultra vy. dk.
844		3012	Khaki Green–med.
843		3364	Pine Green
862		3362	Pine Green–dk.
862		935	Avocado Green–dk.
862		934	Black Avocado Green
898		611	Drab Brown–dk.
380		839	Beige Brown–dk.
382		3371	Black Brown
905		3781	Mocha Brown–dk.
393		3790	Beige Gray–ultra vy. dk.

Step 3: French Knot (1 strand)

891		676	Old Gold–lt.
307		783	Christmas Gold
75		604	Cranberry–lt.
95		554	Violet–lt.
158		747	Sky Blue–vy. lt.
940		3807	Cornflower Blue
393		3790	Beige Gray–ultra vy. dk.

Step 4: Long Stitch (1 strand)

| 894 | | 223 | Shell Pink–med. |
| 393 | | 3790 | Beige Gray–ultra vy. dk. |

Step 5: Beadwork

| | 00557 | Gold |

Stitch Count: 117 width x 204 length

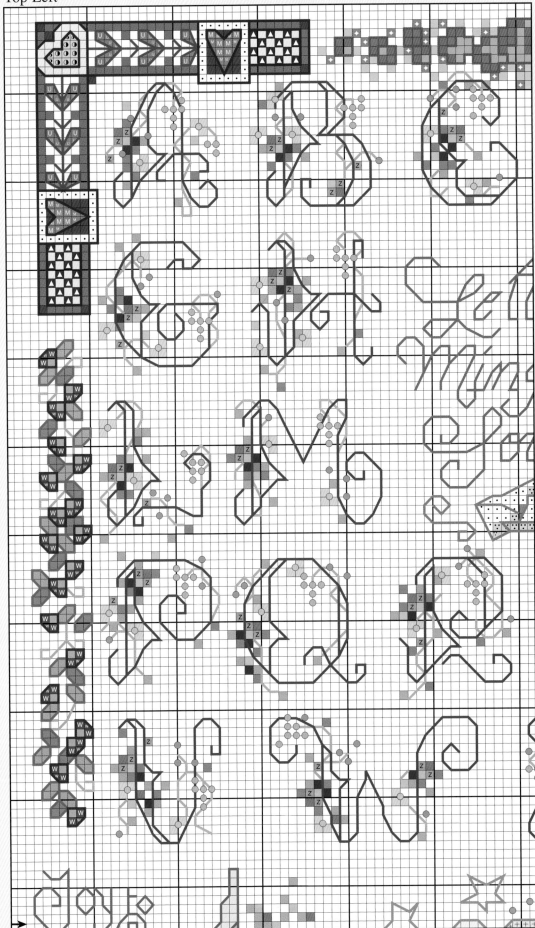

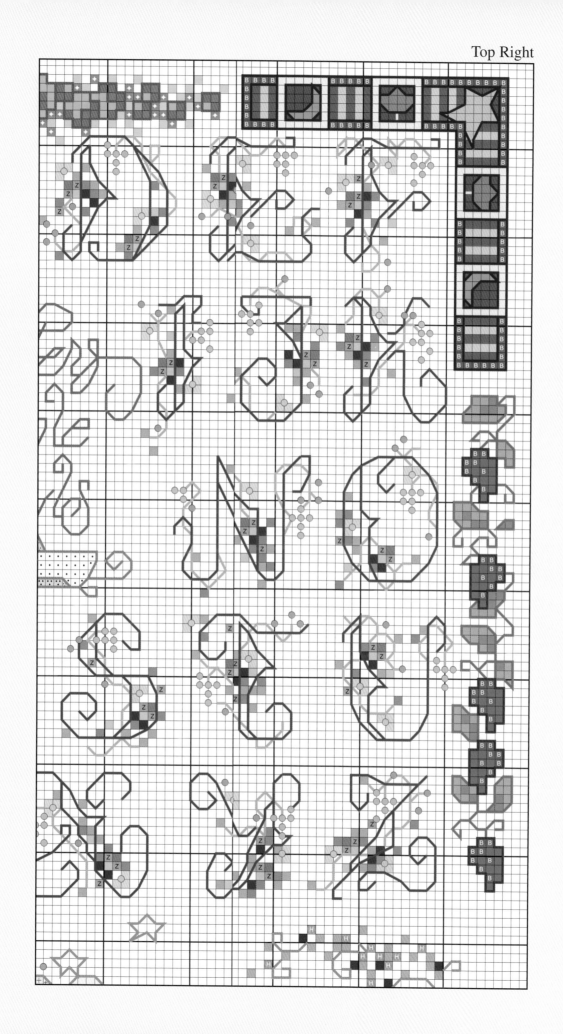

125

Bottom Right

127

Metric Conversion Chart

mm-Millimetres   cm-Centimetres

Inches to Millimetres and Centimetres

inches	mm	cm	inches	cm	inches	cm
⅛	3	0.3	9	22.9	30	76.2
¼	6	0.6	10	25.4	31	78.7
½	13	1.3	12	30.5	33	83.8
⅝	16	1.6	13	33.0	34	86.4
¾	19	1.9	14	35.6	35	88.9
⅞	22	2.2	15	38.1	36	91.4
1	25	2.5	16	40.6	37	94.0
1¼	32	3.2	17	43.2	38	96.5
1½	38	3.8	18	45.7	39	99.1
1¾	44	4.4	19	48.3	40	101.6
2	51	5.1	20	50.8	41	104.1
2½	64	6.4	21	53.3	42	106.7
3	76	7.6	22	55.9	43	109.2
3½	89	8.9	23	58.4	44	111.8
4	102	10.2	24	61.0	45	114.3
4½	114	11.4	25	63.5	46	116.8
5	127	12.7	26	66.0	47	119.4
6	152	15.2	27	68.6	48	121.9
7	178	17.8	28	71.1	49	124.5
8	203	20.3	29	73.7	50	127.0

Index